THE
PLAN

THE PLAN

BARACK OBAMA'S PROMISE TO AMERICA AND HIS PLAN
FOR THE ECONOMY, IRAQ, HEALTH CARE, AND MORE

BARACK OBAMA

pac ps
Pacific Publishing Studio

Copyright 2009 © by Pacific Publishing Studio

Published in the United States by Beacon Hill, an imprint of Pacific Publishing Studio.

www.PacPS.com

ISBN – 978-0-9823756-4-8

To order a copy of this book, visit www.Amazon.com.

Special acknowledgement is made to the following
Cover Photography: Department of Defense
Transcriptions: Pacific Publishing Studio
Contents: www.WhiteHouse.gov, www.Recovery.gov, www.BarackObama.com

Contents

Section Three

Protecting the Nation & Restoring American Values

Section Four

Improving Our Communities

INTRODUCTION

Barack Obama

If there is anyone out there who still doubts that America is a place where all things are possible; who still wonders if the dream of our founders is alive in our time; who still questions the power of our democracy, tonight is your answer.

It's the answer told by lines that stretched around schools and churches in numbers this nation has never seen; by people who waited three hours and four hours, many for the very first time in their lives, because they believed that this time must be different; that their voice could be that difference.

It's the answer spoken by young and old, rich and poor, Democrat and Republican, black, white, Latino, Asian, Native American, gay, straight, disabled and not disabled—Americans who sent a message to the world that we have never been a collection of red states and blue states: we are, and always will be, the United States of America.

It's the answer that led those who have been told for so long by so many to be cynical, and fearful, and doubtful of what we can achieve to put their hands on the arc of history and bend it once more toward the hope of a better day.

It's been a long time coming. But tonight, because of what we did on this day, in this election, at this defining moment, change has come to America.

I just received a very gracious call from Senator McCain. He fought long and hard in this campaign, and he's fought even longer and harder for the country he loves. He has endured sacrifices for America that most of us cannot begin to imagine, and we are better off for the service rendered by this brave and selfless leader. I congratulate him and Governor Palin for all they have achieved, and I look forward to working with them to renew this nation's promise in the months ahead.

I want to thank my partner in this journey, a man who campaigned from his heart and spoke for the men and women he grew up with on the streets of Scranton and rode with on that train home to Delaware, the Vice President-elect of the United States, Joe Biden.

I would not be standing here tonight without the unyielding support of my best friend for the last sixteen years, the rock of our family and the love of my life, our nation's next First Lady, Michelle Obama. Sasha and Malia, I love you both so much, and you have earned the new puppy that's coming with us to the White House. And while she's no longer with us, I know my grandmother is watching, along with the family that made me who I am. I miss them tonight, and know that my debt to them is beyond measure.

To my campaign manager David Plouffe, my chief strategist David Axelrod, and the best campaign team ever assembled in the history of politics—you made this happen, and I am forever grateful for what you've sacrificed to get it done.

But above all, I will never forget who this victory truly belongs to—it belongs to you.

I was never the likeliest candidate for this office. We didn't start with much money or many endorsements. Our campaign was not hatched in the halls of Washington—it began in the backyards of Des Moines and the living rooms of Concord and the front porches of Charleston.

It was built by working men and women who dug into what little savings they had to give five dollars and ten dollars and twenty dollars to this cause. It grew strength from the young people who rejected the myth of their generation's apathy; who left their homes and their families for jobs that offered little pay and less sleep; from the not-so-young people who braved the bitter cold and scorching heat to knock on the doors of perfect strangers; from the millions of Americans who volunteered, and organized, and proved that more than two centuries later, a government of the people, by the people, and for the people has not perished from this Earth.

This is your victory. I know you didn't do this just to win an election, and I know you didn't do it for me. You did it because you understand the enormity of the task that lies ahead. For even as we celebrate tonight, we know the challenges that tomorrow will bring are the greatest of our lifetime—two wars, a planet in peril, the worst financial crisis in a century. Even as we stand here tonight, we know there are brave Americans waking up in the deserts of Iraq and the mountains of Afghanistan to risk their lives for us. There are mothers and fathers who will lie awake after their children fall asleep and wonder how they'll make the mortgage, or pay their doctor's bills, or save enough for college. There is new energy to harness and new jobs to be created; new schools to build and threats to meet and alliances to repair.

The road ahead will be long. Our climb will be steep. We may not get there in one year or even one term, but America—I have never been more hopeful than I am tonight that we will get there. I promise you—we as a people will get there.

There will be setbacks and false starts. There are many who won't agree with every decision or policy I make as President, and we know that government can't solve every problem. But I will always be honest with you about the challenges we face. I will listen to you, especially when we disagree. And above all, I will ask you join in the work of remaking this nation the only way it's been done in America for two-hundred and twenty-one years—block by block, brick by brick, calloused hand by calloused hand.

What began twenty-one months ago in the depths of winter must not end on this autumn night. This victory alone is not the change we seek—it is only the chance for us to make that change. And that cannot happen if we go back to the way things were. It cannot happen without you.

So let us summon a new spirit of patriotism; of service and responsibility where each of us resolves to pitch in and work harder and look after not only ourselves, but each other. Let us remember that if this financial crisis taught us anything, it's that we cannot have a thriving Wall Street while Main Street suffers—in this country, we rise or fall as one nation, as one people.

Let us resist the temptation to fall back on the same partisanship and pettiness and immaturity that has poisoned our politics for so long. Let us remember that it was a man from this state who first carried the banner of the Republican Party to the White House—a party founded on the values of self-reliance, individual liberty, and national unity. Those are values we all share, and while the Democratic Party has won a great victory tonight, we do so with a measure of humility and determination to heal the divides that have held back our progress. As Lincoln said to a nation far more divided than ours, "We are not enemies, but friends...though passion may have strained it must not break our bonds of affection." And to those Americans whose support I have yet to earn—I may not have won your vote, but I hear your voices, I need your help, and I will be your President too.

And to all those watching tonight from beyond our shores, from parliaments and palaces to those who are huddled around radios in the forgotten corners of our world—our stories are singular, but our destiny is shared, and a new dawn of American leadership is at hand.

To those who would tear this world down—we will defeat you. To those who seek peace and security—we support you. And to all those who have wondered if America's beacon still burns as bright—tonight we proved once more that the true strength of our nation comes not from our the might of our arms or the scale of our wealth, but from the enduring power of our ideals: democracy, liberty, opportunity, and unyielding hope.

For that is the true genius of America—that America can change. Our union can be perfected. And what we have already achieved gives us hope for what we can and must achieve tomorrow.

This election had many firsts and many stories that will be told for generations. But one that's on my mind tonight is about a woman who cast her ballot in Atlanta. She's a lot like the millions of others who stood in line to make their voices heard in this election, except for one thing: Ann Nixon Cooper is 106 years old.

She was born just a generation past slavery; a time when there were no cars on the road or planes in the sky; when someone like her couldn't vote for two reasons: because she was a woman and because of the color of her skin.

And tonight, I think about all that she's seen throughout her century in America—the heartache and the hope, the struggle and the progress, the times we were told that we can't, and the people who pressed on with that American creed: Yes we can.

At a time when women's voices were silenced and their hopes dismissed, she lived to see them stand up and speak out and reach for the ballot. Yes we can.

When there was despair in the dust bowl and depression across the land, she saw a nation conquer fear itself with a New Deal, new jobs, and a new sense of common purpose. Yes we can.

When the bombs fell on our harbor and tyranny threatened the world, she was there to witness a generation rise to greatness, and a democracy was saved. Yes we can.

She was there for the buses in Montgomery, the hoses in Birmingham, a bridge in Selma, and a preacher from Atlanta who told a people that, "We Shall Overcome." Yes we can.

A man touched down on the moon, a wall came down in Berlin, a world was connected by our own science and imagination. And this year, in this election, she touched her finger to a screen and cast her vote, because after 106 years in America, through the best of times and the darkest of hours, she knows how America can change. Yes we can.

America, we have come so far. We have seen so much. But there is so much more to do. So tonight, let us ask ourselves—if our children should live to see the next century; if my daughters should be so lucky to live as long as Ann Nixon Cooper, what change will they see? What progress will we have made?

This is our chance to answer that call. This is our moment. This is our time—to put our people back to work and open doors of opportunity for our kids; to restore prosperity and promote the cause of peace; to reclaim the American Dream and reaffirm that fundamental truth—that out of many, we are one; that while we breathe, we hope; and where we are met with cynicism, and doubt, and those who tell us that we can't, we will respond with that timeless creed that sums up the spirit of a people:

Yes We Can. Thank you, God bless you, and may God Bless the United States of America.

Barack Obama
Election Night Victory Speech
Grant Park, Illinois
November 4, 2008

Part One

Restoring the Economy and Meeting Our National Obligations

The Economy

Taxes

Fiscal Policy

Energy and the Environment

Science and Technology

THE ECONOMY

On February 4, 2009, President Obama spoke to the entire Congress to address the country's economic crisis. Excerpts from the speech are transcribed below.

"I know that for many Americans watching right now, the state of our economy is a concern that rises above all others. And rightly so. If you haven't been personally affected by this recession, you probably know someone who has—a friend; a neighbor; a member of your family. You don't need to hear another list of statistics to know that our economy is in crisis, because you live it every day. It's the worry you wake up with and the source of sleepless nights. It's the job you thought you'd retire from but now have lost; the business you built your dreams upon that's now hanging by a thread; the college acceptance letter your child had to put back in the envelope. The impact of this recession is real, and it is everywhere.

But while our economy may be weakened and our confidence shaken, though we are living through difficult and uncertain times, tonight I want every American to know this: We will rebuild, we will recover, and the United States of America will emerge stronger than before.

The weight of this crisis will not determine the destiny of this nation. The answers to our problems don't lie beyond our reach. They exist in our laboratories and our universities; in our fields and our factories; in the imaginations of our entrepreneurs and the pride of the hardest-working people on Earth. Those qualities that have made America the greatest force of progress and prosperity in human history we still possess in ample measure. What is required now is for this country to pull together, confront boldly the challenges we face, and take responsibility for our future once more.

Now, if we're honest with ourselves, we'll admit that for too long, we have not always met these responsibilities—as a government or as a people. I say this not to lay blame or to look backwards, but because it is only by understanding how we arrived at this moment that we'll be able to lift ourselves out of this predicament.

The fact is our economy did not fall into decline overnight. Nor did all of our problems begin when the housing market collapsed or the stock market sank. We have known for decades that our survival depends on finding new sources of energy. Yet we import more oil today than ever before. The cost of health care eats up more and more of our savings each year, yet we keep delaying reform. Our children will compete for jobs in a global economy that too many of our schools do not prepare them for. And though all these challenges went unsolved, we still managed to spend more money and pile up more debt, both as individuals and through our government, than ever before.

In other words, we have lived through an era where too often short-term gains were prized over long-term prosperity; where we failed to look beyond the next payment, the next quarter, or the next election. A surplus became an excuse to transfer wealth to the wealthy instead of an opportunity to invest in our future. Regulations were gutted for the sake of a quick profit at the expense of a healthy market. People bought homes they knew they couldn't afford from banks and lenders who pushed those bad loans anyway. And all the while, critical debates and difficult decisions were put off for some other time on some other day.

Well that day of reckoning has arrived, and the time to take charge of our future is here.

Now is the time to act boldly and wisely—to not only revive this economy, but to build a new foundation for lasting prosperity. Now is the time to jumpstart job creation, re-start lending, and invest in areas like energy, health care, and education that will grow our economy, even as we make hard choices to bring our deficit down. That is what my economic agenda is designed to do, and that is what I'd like to talk to you about tonight.

It's an agenda that begins with jobs.

As soon as I took office, I asked this Congress to send me a recovery plan by President's Day that would put people back to work and put money in their pockets. Not because I believe in bigger government—I don't. Not because I'm not mindful of the massive debt we've inherited—I am. I called for action because the failure to do so would have cost more jobs and caused more hardship. In fact, a failure to act would have worsened our long-term deficit by assuring weak economic growth for years. And that's why I pushed for quick action. And tonight, I am grateful that this Congress delivered, and pleased to say that the American Recovery and Reinvestment Act is now law.

Over the next two years, this plan will save or create 3.5 million jobs. More than 90 percent of these jobs will be in the private sector—jobs rebuilding our roads and bridges; constructing wind turbines and solar panels; laying broadband and expanding mass transit.

Because of this plan, there are teachers who can now keep their jobs and educate our kids. Health care professionals can continue caring for our sick. There are 57 police officers who are still on the streets of Minneapolis tonight because this plan prevented the layoffs their department was about to make.

Because of this plan, 95 percent of working households in America will receive a tax cut—a tax cut that you will see in your paychecks beginning on April 1st.

Because of this plan, families who are struggling to pay tuition costs will receive a $2,500 tax credit for all four years of college. And Americans who have lost their jobs in this recession will be able to receive extended unemployment benefits and continued health care coverage to help them weather this storm.

Now, I know there are some in this chamber and watching at home who are skeptical of whether this plan will work. And I understand that skepticism. Here in Washington, we've all seen how quickly good intentions can turn into broken promises and wasteful spending. And with a plan of this scale comes enormous responsibility to get it right...

...I have told each of my Cabinet, as well as mayors and governors across the country, that they will be held accountable by me and the American people for every dollar they spend. I've appointed a proven and aggressive Inspector General to ferret out any and all cases of waste and fraud. And we have created a new website called recovery.gov so that every American can find out how and where their money is being spent.

So the recovery plan we passed is the first step in getting our economy back on track. But it is just the first step. Because even if we manage this plan flawlessly, there will be no real recovery unless we clean up the credit crisis that has severely weakened our financial system.

I want to speak plainly and candidly about this issue tonight, because every American should know that it directly affects you and your family's well-being. You should also know that the money you've deposited in banks across the country is safe; your insurance is secure; you can rely on the continued operation of our financial system. That's not the source of concern.

The concern is that if we do not restart lending in this country, our recovery will be choked off before it even begins.

You see, the flow of credit is the lifeblood of our economy. The ability to get a loan is how you finance the purchase of everything from a home to a car to a college education, how stores stock their shelves, farms buy equipment, and businesses make payroll.

But credit has stopped flowing the way it should. Too many bad loans from the housing crisis have made their way onto the books of too many banks. And with so much debt and so little confidence, these banks are now fearful of lending out any more money to households, to businesses, or even to each other. And when there is no lending, families can't afford to buy homes or cars. So businesses are forced to make layoffs. Our economy suffers even more, and credit dries up even further.

That is why this Administration is moving swiftly and aggressively to break this destructive cycle, to restore confidence, and restart lending.

And we will do so in several ways. First, we are creating a new lending fund that represents the largest effort ever to help provide auto loans, college loans, and small business loans to the consumers and entrepreneurs who keep this economy running.

Second, we have launched a housing plan that will help responsible families facing the threat of foreclosure lower their monthly payments and refinance their mortgages. It's a plan that won't help speculators or that neighbor down the street who bought a house he could never hope to afford, but it will help millions of Americans who are struggling with declining home values—Americans who will now be able to take advantage of the lower interest rates that this plan has already helped to bring about. In fact, the average family who refinances today can save nearly $2,000 per year on their mortgage.

Third, we will act with the full force of the federal government to ensure that the major banks that Americans depend on have enough confidence and enough money to lend even in more difficult times. And when we learn that a major bank has serious problems, we will hold accountable those responsible, force the necessary adjustments, provide the support to clean up their balance sheets, and assure the continuity of a strong, viable institution that can serve our people and our economy.

I understand that on any given day, Wall Street may be more comforted by an approach that gives bank bailouts with no strings attached, and that holds nobody accountable for their reckless decisions. But such an approach won't solve the problem. And our goal is to quicken the day when we restart lending to the American people and American business, and end this crisis once and for all.

And I intend to hold these banks fully accountable for the assistance they receive, and this time, they will have to clearly demonstrate how taxpayer dollars result in more lending for the American taxpayer. This time, CEOs won't be able to use taxpayer money to pad their paychecks, or buy fancy drapes, or disappear on a private jet. Those days are over.

Still, this plan will require significant resources from the federal government—and, yes, probably more than we've already set aside. But while the cost of action will be great, I can assure you that the cost of inaction will be far greater, for it could result in an economy that sputters along for not months or years, but perhaps a decade. That would be worse for our deficit, worse for business, worse for you, and worse for the next generation. And I refuse to let that happen.

Now, I understand that when the last Administration asked this Congress to provide assistance for struggling banks, Democrats and Republicans alike were infuriated by the mismanagement and the results that followed. So were the American taxpayers. So was I. So I know how unpopular it is to be seen as helping banks right now, especially when everyone is suffering in part from their bad decisions. I promise you—I get it.

But I also know that in a time of crisis, we cannot afford to govern out of anger, or yield to the politics of the moment. My job—our job—is to solve the problem. Our job is to govern with a sense of responsibility. I will not send—I will not spend a single penny for the purpose of rewarding a single Wall Street executive, but I will do whatever it takes to help the small business that can't pay its workers, or the family that has saved and still can't get a mortgage.

That's what this is about. It's not about helping banks—it's about helping people. It's not about helping banks; it's about helping people. Because when credit is available again, that young family can finally buy a new home. And then some company will hire workers to build it. And then those workers will have money to spend. And if they can get a loan, too, maybe they'll finally buy that car, or open their own business. Investors will return to the market, and American families will see their retirement secured once more. Slowly, but surely, confidence will return, and our economy will recover....

...My budget does not attempt to solve every problem or address every issue. It reflects the stark reality of what we've inherited—a trillion-dollar deficit, a financial crisis, and a costly recession.

Given these realities, everyone in this chamber—Democrats and Republicans—will have to sacrifice some worthy priorities for which there are no dollars. And that includes me.

But that does not mean we can afford to ignore our long-term challenges. I reject the view that says our problems will simply take care of themselves; that says government has no role in laying the foundation for our common prosperity.

For history tells a different story. History reminds us that at every moment of economic upheaval and transformation, this nation has responded with bold action and big ideas. In the midst of civil war, we laid railroad tracks from one coast to another that spurred commerce and industry. From the turmoil of the Industrial Revolution came a system of public high schools that prepared our citizens for a new age. In the wake of war and depression, the GI Bill sent a generation to college and created the largest middle class in history. And a twilight struggle for freedom led to a nation of highways, an American on the moon, and an explosion of technology that still shapes our world.

In each case, government didn't supplant private enterprise; it catalyzed private enterprise. It created the conditions for thousands of entrepreneurs and new businesses to adapt and to thrive.

We are a nation that has seen promise amid peril, and claimed opportunity from ordeal. Now we must be that nation again. That is why, even as it cuts back on programs we don't need, the budget I submit will invest in the three areas that are absolutely critical to our economic future: energy, health care, and education.

It begins with energy.

We know the country that harnesses the power of clean, renewable energy will lead the 21st century. And yet, it is China that has launched the largest effort in history to make their economy energy-efficient. We invented solar technology, but we've fallen behind countries like Germany and Japan in producing it. New plug-in hybrids roll off our assembly lines, but they will run on batteries made in Korea.

Well, I do not accept a future where the jobs and industries of tomorrow take root beyond our borders—and I know you don't, either. It is time for America to lead again."

President Obama has stated that if we do not act quickly, our recession could linger for years—and America could lose the competitive edge that has served as the foundation for our strength and standing in the world.

To rescue the economy and prevent economic failure, the President has signed into law the American Recovery and Reinvestment Act, which will jumpstart job creation and long-term growth. The plan includes ambitious goals with the following targets:

- Create or save more than 3.5 million jobs over the next two years
- Take a big step toward computerizing Americans' health records, reducing medical errors and saving billions in health care costs
- Revive the renewable energy industry and provide the capital over the next three years to eventually double domestic renewable energy capacity
- Undertake the largest weatherization program in history by modernizing 75 percent of federal building space and more than one million homes
- Increase college affordability for seven million students by funding the shortfall in Pell Grants, increasing the maximum award level by $500, and providing a new higher education tax cut to nearly four million students
- As part of the $150 billion investment in new infrastructure, enact the largest increase in funding of our nation's roads, bridges, and mass transit systems since the creation of the national highway system in the 1950s
- Provide an $800 Making Work Pay tax credit for 129 million working households, and cut taxes for the

families of millions of children through an expansion of the Child Tax Credit

- Require unprecedented levels of transparency, oversight, and accountability

In the face of an economic crisis, the magnitude of which we have not seen since the Great Depression, the American Recovery and Reinvestment Act represents a strategic and significant investment in our country's future.

The Act will aim to create or save three to four million jobs, 90 percent of them in the private sector. It will provide more than $150 billion to low-income and vulnerable households—spurring increased economic activity that will save or create more than one million jobs.

Barack Obama believes these measures are necessary to help the millions of families whose lives have been upended by the economic crisis. He hopes this Act will do more than provide short-term stimulus. By modernizing our health care, improving our schools, modernizing our infrastructure, and investing in the clean energy technologies of the future, the Act should lay the foundation for a robust and sustainable 21st century economy.

TAXES

President Obama's tax plan delivers broad-based tax relief to middle class families and cuts taxes for the small businesses and companies that create jobs in America. It also aims to restore fairness to our tax code and return to fiscal responsibility. Coupled with Obama's commitment to invest in key areas like healthcare, clean energy, innovation, and education, his tax plan will help restore bottom-up economic growth that creates good jobs in America and empowers all families to achieve the American dream.

Obama's Tax Policy promises to:
- Cut taxes for 95 percent of workers and their families with a tax cut of $500 for workers or $1,000 for working couples.
- Provide generous tax cuts for low and middle-income seniors, homeowners, the uninsured, and families sending a child to college or looking to save and accumulate wealth.
- Eliminate capital gains taxes for small businesses, cut corporate taxes for firms that invest and create jobs in the United States, and provide tax credits to reduce the cost of healthcare and to reward investments in innovation.
- Dramatically simplify taxes by consolidating existing tax credits, eliminating the need for millions of senior citizens to file tax forms, and enabling as many as 40 million middle-class Americans to do their own taxes in less than five minutes without an accountant.

- Middle class families will see their taxes cut, and no family making less than $250,000 will see their taxes increase. The typical middle class family will receive well over $1,000 in tax relief under the plan and will pay tax rates that are 20 percent lower than they faced under President Reagan.
- Families making more than $250,000 will pay either the same or lower tax rates than they paid in the 1990s. Obama will ask the wealthiest two percent of families to give back a portion of the tax cuts they have received during the Bush administration to ensure we are restoring fairness and returning to fiscal responsibility. And no family will pay higher tax rates than they would have paid in the 1990s.
- Obama's plan will cut taxes overall, reducing revenues to below the levels that prevailed under Ronald Reagan (less than 18.2 percent of GDP). The plan is a net tax cut—his tax relief for middle class families is larger than the revenue raised by his tax changes for families over $250,000. Coupled with his commitment to cut unnecessary spending, Obama will pay for this tax relief while bringing down the budget deficit.

WHO	TAX CUT
Married couple making $75,000 with two children, one of whom is in college	**$3,700** (includes $1,000 Making Work Pay; $500 universal mortgage credit; and $4,000 college credit net of current college credits)
Married couple making $90,000	**$1,000** ($1,000 Making Work Pay tax credit)
Single parent making $40,000 with two young children and childcare expenses	**$2,100** (includes $500 Making Work Pay; $500 universal mortgage credit; and $1,100 from expansion of the child care tax credit)
70-year-old widow making	$1,900

$35,000	(reflects elimination of income taxes for seniors earning under $50,000)

Source: Calculations based on IRS Statistics of Income. Tax savings is conservative. It does not account for up to $500 in savings from expanded Savers Credit and the $2,500 in savings per family from the Obama healthcare plan.

FISCAL POLICY

"The cost of our debt is one of the fastest growing expenses in the federal budget. This rising debt is a hidden domestic enemy, robbing our cities and states of critical investments in infrastructure like bridges, ports, and levees; robbing our families and our children of critical investments in education and health care reform; robbing our seniors of the retirement and health security they have counted on. . . . If Washington were serious about honest tax relief in this country, we'd see an effort to reduce our national debt by returning to responsible fiscal policies."
Barack Obama, Speech in the U.S. Senate, March 13, 2006

President Obama has been a strong advocate for sound budget practices and the reduction of wasteful spending in Washington. He is committed to fiscal transparency and accountability and ensuring that all new tax cuts and spending commitments are paid for without burdening future generations with excessive debt. President Obama will fight to modernize government policies to secure and expand the middle class. He will keep taxes low for middle class and low-income families while making the necessary investments to grow the American economy.

Obama plans to achieve his goal by restoring fiscal discipline to Washington and by making the tax system fair and efficient.

Reinstate PAYGO Rules
President Obama believes that a critical step in restoring fiscal discipline is enforcing pay-as-you-go (PAYGO) budgeting rules. These rules will require new spending

commitments or tax changes to be paid for by cuts to other programs or new revenue.

Reverse Tax Cuts for the Wealthy
Obama's plan will protect tax cuts for poor and middle class families, but it will reverse most of the Bush tax cuts for the wealthiest taxpayers.

Cut Pork Barrel Spending
As a Senator, President Obama introduced and passed bipartisan legislation to require more disclosure and transparency for special-interest earmarks. Obama believes that spending that cannot withstand public scrutiny cannot be justified. He promises to slash earmarks to no greater than 1994 levels and ensure all spending decisions are open to the public.

Make Spending More Accountable and Efficient
Unlike in previous years, federal contracts over $25,000 will be competitively bid. Obama's plan will also increase the efficiency of government programs through better use of technology, stronger management that demands account-ability, and by leveraging the government's high-volume purchasing power to get lower prices.

End Wasteful Government Spending
Wasteful, obsolete federal government programs that make no financial sense will no longer be funded. Obama has called for an end to subsidies for oil and gas companies that are enjoying record profits, as well as the elimination of subsidies to the private student loan industry, which has repeatedly used unethical business practices. Obama also plans to tackle wasteful spending in the Medicare program.

End Tax Haven Abuse

Building on his bipartisan work in the Senate, Obama will give the Treasury Department the tools it needs to stop the abuse of tax shelters and offshore tax havens and help close the $350 billion tax gap between taxes owed and taxes paid.

Close Special Interest/Corporate Loopholes

Obama wants to level the playing field for all businesses by eliminating special interest loopholes and deductions, such as those for the oil and gas industry.

ENERGY & THE ENVIRONMENT

"Thanks to our recovery plan, we will double this nation's supply of renewable energy in the next three years. We've also made the largest investment in basic research funding in American history—an investment that will spur not only new discoveries in energy, but breakthroughs in medicine and science and technology.

We will soon lay down thousands of miles of power lines that can carry new energy to cities and towns across this country. And we will put Americans to work making our homes and buildings more efficient so that we can save billions of dollars on our energy bills.

But to truly transform our economy, to protect our security, and save our planet from the ravages of climate change, we need to ultimately make clean, renewable energy the profitable kind of energy. So I ask this Congress to send me legislation that places a market-based cap on carbon pollution and drives the production of more renewable energy in America. That's what we need. And to support—to support that innovation, we will invest $15 billion a year to develop technologies like wind power and solar power, advanced biofuels, clean coal, and more efficient cars and trucks built right here in America.

Speaking of our auto industry, everyone recognizes that years of bad decision-making and a global recession have pushed our automakers to the brink. We should not, and will not, protect them from their own bad practices. But we are committed to the goal of a retooled, reimagined auto industry that can compete and win. Millions of jobs depend on it.

Scores of communities depend on it. And I believe the nation that invented the automobile cannot walk away from it.

None of this will come without cost, nor will it be easy. But this is America. We don't do what's easy. We do what's necessary to move this country forward."
Barack Obama, February 4, 2009

The energy challenges our country faces are severe and have gone unaddressed for far too long. Our addiction to foreign oil doesn't just undermine our national security and wreak havoc on our environment—it cripples our economy and strains the budgets of working families all across America. President Obama promises to invest in alternative and renewable energy, end our addiction to foreign oil, address the global climate crisis, and create millions of new jobs.

The goals of the Obama comprehensive New Energy for America Plan address short term relief as well as long term needs.

Short Term Relief

Energy Rebate
Obama will institute a windfall profits tax on record oil company profits. This money will then be used to provide rebates to Americans worth $500 for an individual and $1,000 for a married couple.

The rebate will be designed to offset the increase in gas prices for a working family or to pay for the increase in winter heating bills.

Reduce Energy Speculation

Experts believe that loopholes in trading regulations have contributed to the rising price of oil. Barack Obama's plan will close loopholes and increase transparency to bring oil prices down.

Long Term Solutions

Obama's energy plan will tackle the challenges we face with climate change as well as our dependency on oil. His goal is to make the U.S. a world leader on climate change.

Reduce Greenhouse Gas Emissions

Barack Obama supports implementation of an economy-wide cap-and-trade system to reduce carbon emissions. The cap-and-trade policy will ensure that all industries pay for every ton of emissions they release.

The money generated by the policy will be used in several areas:

- Clean energy development
- Development of the next generation of bio-fuels and clean energy vehicles
- Funding to state and federal land and wildlife managers to deal with the effects of global warming
- Relief to help families and communities transition to a new low carbon economy
- Make investments that will reduce our dependence on foreign oil

Invest In A Clean Energy Economy

Barack Obama promises to invest $150 billion over ten years. His goal is to improve our energy crisis in several areas:

- Commercialization of plug-in hybrids
- Development of renewable energy
- Improve energy efficiency
- Invest in low emissions coal plants
- Advance the next generation of bio-fuels and fuel infrastructure
- Begin transition to a new digital electricity grid

Obama believes that with focus on energy and investment into the skills of our manufacturing workforce, his plan will create 5 million new private sector jobs.

Improve Fuel Efficiency

Within ten years, Obama's plan is to save more oil than we currently import from the Middle East and Venezuela combined. He will accomplish this through several efforts:

- Increase fuel economy standards by 4 percent per each year
- Invest in developing advanced vehicles
- Put 1 million plug-in electric vehicles on the road by 2015 that get up to 150 miles per gallon
- Provide a $7,000 tax credit for the purchase of advanced technology vehicles
- Convert the entire White House fleet to plug-ins
- By 2012, half of all cars purchased by the federal government will be plug-in hybrids or all-electric

Promote the Supply of Domestic Energy

Obama promises to focus on several areas he believes are the key to leveraging America's own supply of energy based resources:

- Use it or lose it: If energy companies continue to ignore over one-hundred million acres of land and offshore areas they have been given to drill in, they will lose them.
- Production of oil and natural gas: Early identification of obstacles that might delay drilling in key domestic areas.
- Facilitate construction of the Alaska natural gas pipeline.
- Improve production at our existing oil fields.

SCIENCE & TECHNOLOGY

"Let us be the generation that reshapes our economy to compete in the digital age. Let's set high standards for our schools and give them the resources they need to succeed. Let's recruit a new army of teachers, and give them better pay and more support in exchange for more accountability. Let's make college more affordable, and let's invest in scientific research, and let's lay down broadband lines through the heart of inner cities and rural towns all across America."
Barack Obama, Springfield, IL February 10, 2007

President Obama understands the immense transformative power of technology and innovation and how they can improve the lives of Americans. He has promised to work to ensure the full and free exchange of information through an open Internet and use technology to create a more transparent and connected democracy. He will encourage the deployment of modern communication infrastructure to improve America's competitiveness and employ technology to solve our nation's most pressing problems—including improving clean energy, healthcare costs, and public safety.

Obama will ensure the full and free exchange of ideas through an open internet and diverse media outlets in four key ways:

Protect the Openness of the Internet
Support the principle of network neutrality to preserve the benefits of open competition on the Internet.

Encourage Diversity in Media Ownership

Encourage diversity in the ownership of broadcast media, promote the development of new media outlets for expression of diverse viewpoints, and clarify the public interest obligations of broadcasters who occupy the nation's spectrum.

Protect Children and Preserve the First Amendment

Give parents the tools and information they need to control what their children see on television and the Internet in ways fully consistent with the First Amendment. Support tough penalties, increase enforcement resources and forensic tools for law enforcement, and encourage collaboration between law enforcement and the private sector to identify and prosecute people who try to exploit children online.

Safeguard our Right to Privacy

Strengthen privacy protections for the digital age and harness the power of technology to hold government and business accountable for violations of personal privacy.

President Obama's goal to create a transparent and connected democracy will happen through:

Opening Government to its Citizens

Cutting-edge technologies will be used to create a new level of transparency, accountability, and participation for America's citizens.

Bringing Government into the 21st Century

Technology will be used to reform government and improve the exchange of information between the federal government and citizens while ensuring the security of our networks. Obama promises to appoint the nation's first Chief

Technology Officer (CTO) to ensure the safety of our networks and lead an interagency effort, working with chief technology and chief information officers of each of the federal agencies to ensure that they use best-in-class technologies and share best practices.

Next-Generation Broadband
Obama will work towards true broadband in every community in America through a combination of reform of the Universal Service Fund, better use of the nation's wireless spectrum, promotion of next-generation facilities, technologies and applications, and new tax and loan incentives. America should lead the world in broadband penetration and Internet access.

Improve America's Competitiveness

President Obama has offered his commitment to keeping America at the forefront of technology and innovation. He has promised to ensure that America stays competitive in the global economy by pressing the following priorities:

Promote American Businesses Abroad
Support a trade policy that ensures our goods and services are treated fairly in foreign markets. Fight for fair treatment of our companies abroad.

Invest in the Sciences
Double federal funding for basic research over ten years, in order to change the posture of our federal government to one that embraces science and technology.

Invest in University-Based Research

Expand research initiatives at American colleges and universities. Provide new research grants to the most outstanding early-career researchers in the country.

Make the R&D Tax Credit Permanent

Invest in a skilled research and development workforce and technology infrastructure. Make the Research and Development tax credit permanent so that firms can rely on it when making decisions to invest in domestic R&D over multi-year timeframes.

Ensure Competitive Markets

Foster a business and regulatory landscape in which entrepreneurs and small businesses can thrive, start-ups can launch, and all enterprises can compete effectively while investors and consumers are protected against bad actors that cross the line. Reinvigorate antitrust enforcement to ensure that capitalism works for consumers.

Protect American Intellectual Property Abroad

Work to ensure intellectual property is protected in foreign markets, and promote greater cooperation on international standards that allow our technologies to compete everywhere.

Protect American Intellectual Property at Home

Update and reform our copyright and patent systems to promote civic discourse, innovation, and investment while ensuring that intellectual property owners are fairly treated.

Reform the Patent System

Ensure that our patent laws protect legitimate rights while not stifling innovation and collaboration. Give the

Patent and Trademark Office (PTO) the resources to improve patent quality and open up the patent process to citizen review in order to foster an environment that encourages innovation. Reduce uncertainty and wasteful litigation that is currently a significant drag on innovation.

Restore Scientific Integrity to the White House

Restore the basic principle that government decisions should be based on the best-available, scientifically-valid evidence and not on ideological predispositions.

College Aid for Math and Science Students

Launch an online database to give potential future scientists access to information about financial aid opportunities available in science and technology fields through the federal government and public or private resources.

Increase Science and Math Graduates

Improve science and math education in K-12 to prepare more students for these studies in college. Work to increase our number of science and engineering graduates and encourage undergraduates studying math and science to pursue graduate studies.

Lifelong Re-training of Adults

Reauthorize the Workforce Investment Act, and increase resources for community colleges and lifelong learning initiatives to ensure our citizens can continue to gain new skills throughout their lifetimes. Modernize and expand the existing system of trade adjustment assistance to include service sector workers hurt by changing trade patterns. Create flexible education accounts that workers can use for re-training.

Build a Reliable Safety Net

Through his proposals on portable health care, retirement savings accounts, and expanded unemployment insurance, Obama promises to work for programs that will help Americans who face job transitions in a fierce global economy.

Employ Science, Technology, and Innovation to Solve Our Nation's Most Pressing Problems

Twenty-first century technology and telecommunications have flattened communications as well as labor markets and have contributed to a period of unprecedented innovation, making us more productive, connected global citizens. By maximizing the power of technology, Obama wants to strengthen the quality and affordability of our health care, advance climate-friendly energy development and deployment, and improve education throughout the country. He believes this will ensure that America remains the world's leader in technology.

Lower Health Care Costs with Information Technology

Use health information technology to lower the cost of health care. Invest $10 billion a year over the next five years to move the U.S. health care system to a broad adoption of standards-based electronic health information systems, including electronic health records.

Invest in Climate-Friendly Energy

Invest $150 billion over the next ten years to enable American engineers, scientists, and entrepreneurs to advance the next generation of bio-fuels and fuel infrastructure, accelerate the commercialization of plug-in hybrids, promote development of commercial-scale renewable energy, and begin the transition to a new digital electricity grid. This investment will transform the economy and create 5 million new jobs.

Modernize Public Safety Networks

Spur the development and deployment of new technologies to promote interoperability, broadband access, and more effective communications among first responders and emergency response systems.

Advance the Biomedical Research Field

Support investments in biomedical research as well as medical education and training in health-related fields. Fund biomedical research, and make it more efficient by improving coordination both within government and across government /private/non-profit partnerships.

Supporting Stem Cell Research

President Obama believes that American scientists should explore the potential of stem cells to treat the millions of people suffering from debilitating and life-threatening diseases. Obama is a co-sponsor of the Stem Cell Research Enhancement Act of 2007, which will allow research of human embryonic stem cells derived from embryos donated (with consent) from in vitro fertilization clinics. These embryos must be deemed in excess and created based solely for the purpose of fertility treatment.

Science

In the past, government funding for scientific research has yielded innovations that have improved the landscape of American life—technologies like the Internet, digital photography, bar codes, Global Positioning Systems, laser surgery, and chemotherapy. At one time, educational competition with the Soviets fostered the creativity that put a man on the moon. Though we face a new set of challenges, including energy security, HIV/AIDS, and climate change, the United States is losing its scientific dominance.

Among industrialized nations, our country's scores on international science and math tests rank in the bottom third and bottom fifth, respectively. Over the last three decades, federal funding for the physical, mathematical, and engineering sciences has declined at a time when other countries are substantially increasing their own research budgets. President Obama believes that federally funded scientific research should play an important role in advancing science and technology in the classroom and in the lab.

Part Two

Improving the Lives of Americans

Health Care

Education

Family

Women

Social Security and Medicare

HEALTH CARE

"I think it should be a right for every American. In a country as wealthy as ours, for us to have people who are going bankrupt because they can't pay their medical bills—for my mother to die of cancer at the age of 53 and have to spend the last months of her life in the hospital room arguing with insurance companies because they're saying that this may be a pre-existing condition and they don't have to pay her treatment, there's something fundamentally wrong about that."
Barack Obama, October 7, 2008

"This is a cost that now causes a bankruptcy in America every 30 seconds. By the end of the year, it could cause 1.5 million Americans to lose their homes. In the last eight years, premiums have grown four times faster than wages. And in each of these years, 1 million more Americans have lost their health insurance. It is one of the major reasons why small businesses close their doors and corporations ship jobs overseas. And it's one of the largest and fastest-growing parts of our budget.

Given these facts, we can no longer afford to put health care reform on hold. We can't afford to do it. It's time.

Already, we've done more to advance the cause of health care reform in the last 30 days than we've done in the last decade. When it was days old, this Congress passed a law to provide and protect health insurance for 11 million American children whose parents work full-time. Our recovery plan will invest in electronic health records and new technology that will reduce errors, bring down costs, ensure privacy, and save lives. It will launch a new effort to conquer a disease that has touched the life of nearly every American, including me, by seeking a cure for cancer in our time. And it makes the largest investment ever in preventive care, because that's one of the best ways to keep our people healthy and our costs under control.

This budget builds on these reforms. It includes a historic commitment to comprehensive health care reform—a down payment on the principle that we must have quality, affordable health care for every American. It's a commitment—it's a commitment that's paid for in part by efficiencies in our system that are long overdue. And it's a step we must take if we hope to bring down our deficit in the years to come.

Now, there will be many different opinions and ideas about how to achieve reform, and that's why I'm bringing together businesses and workers, doctors and health care providers, Democrats and Republicans to begin work on this issue next week.

I suffer no illusions that this will be an easy process. Once again, it will be hard. But I also know that nearly a century after Teddy Roosevelt first called for reform, the cost of our health care has weighed down our economy and our conscience long enough. So let there be no doubt: Health care reform cannot wait, it must not wait, and it will not wait another year."
Barack Obama, February 24, 2009

On health care reform, the American people are too often given a choice of two extremes: government-run health care with higher taxes or insurance companies that operate without rules or regulation. President Obama's plan concludes that both of these extremes are wrong, and instead, proposes a way to strengthen employer coverage, makes insurance companies accountable, and ensures patient choice of doctor and care without government interference.

The plan provides affordable, accessible health care for all Americans, builds on the existing health care system, and uses existing providers, doctors, and plans to ensure its success. Patients will be able to make health care decisions with their doctors, instead of being blocked by insurance company bureaucrats.

Under the plan, if you like your current health insurance, nothing will change, except for your costs, which will go down by as much as $2,500 per year. If you *don't* have health insurance, you will have a choice of new, affordable health insurance options. More details of the plan are outlined below:

People and Businesses First
- Require insurance companies to cover pre-existing conditions so all Americans, regardless of their health status or history, can get comprehensive benefits at fair and stable premiums.
- Create a new Small Business Health Tax Credit to help small businesses provide affordable health insurance to their employees.
- Lower costs for businesses by covering a portion of the catastrophic health costs they pay, in return for lower premiums for employees.

- Prevent insurers from overcharging doctors for their malpractice insurance and invest in proven strategies to reduce preventable medical errors.
- Improve employer contributions by requiring large employers, that do not offer coverage or make a meaningful contribution to the cost of quality health coverage for their employees, to contribute a percentage of payroll toward the costs of their employees' health care.
- Establish a National Health Insurance Exchange with a range of private insurance options that will allow individuals and small businesses to buy affordable health coverage. Included will be a new public plan based on the same benefits available to members of Congress. That will allow individuals and small businesses to buy affordable health coverage.
- Ensure that everyone who needs it will receive a tax credit for their premiums.

Reduce Costs and Save Money
- Lower drug costs by allowing the importation of safe medicines from other developed countries.
- Increase the use of generic drugs in public programs and take on drug companies that block cheaper generic medicines from the market.
- Require hospitals to collect and report health care costs and quality data.
- Reduce the costs of catastrophic illnesses for employers and their employees.
- Reform the insurance market to increase competition by taking on anticompetitive activity that drives up prices but don't improve the quality of care.

Obama's plan to promote public health will also require coverage of preventive services such as cancer screenings, as well as increased state and local preparedness for terrorist attacks and natural disasters.

President Obama intends to pay for his $50 - $65 billion health care reform effort by rolling back the Bush tax cuts for Americans earning more than $250,000 per year and retaining the estate tax at its 2009 level.

Promote AIDS Prevention

President Obama will develop and begin to implement a comprehensive national HIV/AIDS strategy that includes all federal agencies. The strategy will be designed to reduce HIV infections, increase access to care, and reduce HIV-related health disparities.

The President will support common sense approaches including: age-appropriate sex education that includes information about contraception, combating infection within our prison population through education and contraception, and distributing contraceptives through our public health system.

The President also supports lifting the federal ban on needle exchange, which could dramatically reduce rates of infection among drug users. President Obama has also been willing to confront the stigma—often tied to homophobia—that continues to surround HIV/AIDS.

EDUCATION

"In a global economy, where the most valuable skill you can sell is your knowledge, a good education is no longer just a pathway to opportunity—it is a prerequisite.

Right now, three-quarters of the fastest-growing occupations require more than a high school diploma. And yet, just over half of our citizens have that level of education. We have one of the highest high school dropout rates of any industrialized nation. And half of the students who begin college never finish.

This is a prescription for economic decline, because we know the countries that out-teach us today will out-compete us tomorrow. That is why it will be the goal of this Administration to ensure that every child has access to a complete and competitive education—from the day they are born to the day they begin a career. That is a promise we have to make to the children of America.

Already, we've made an historic investment in education through the economic recovery plan. We've dramatically expanded early childhood education and will continue to improve its quality, because we know that the most formative learning comes in those first years of life. We've made college affordable for nearly seven million more students-seven million. And we have provided the resources necessary to prevent painful cuts and teacher layoffs that would set back our children's progress.

But we know that our schools don't just need more resources. They need more reform. That is why this budget creates new teachers—new incentives for teacher performance; pathways for advancement, and rewards for success. We'll invest in innovative programs that are already helping schools meet high standards and close achievement gaps. And we will expand our commitment to charter schools.

It is our responsibility as lawmakers and as educators to make this system work. But it is the responsibility of every citizen to participate in it. So tonight, I ask every American to commit to at least one year or more of higher education or career training. This can be community college or a four-year school; vocational training or an apprenticeship. But whatever the training may be, every American will need to get more than a high school diploma.

And dropping out of high school is no longer an option. It's not just quitting on yourself, it's quitting on your country— and this country needs and values the talents of every American. That's why we will support—we will provide the support necessary for all young Americans to complete college and meet a new goal: By 2020, America will once again have the highest proportion of college graduates in the world. That's is a goal we can meet.

Now, I know that the price of tuition is higher than ever, which is why if you are willing to volunteer in your neighborhood or give back to your community or serve your country, we will make sure that you can afford a higher education...

...Education policies will open the doors of opportunity for our children. But it is up to us to ensure they walk through them. In the end, there is no program or policy that can substitute for a parent—for a mother or father who will attend those parent/teacher conferences, or help with homework, or turn off the TV, put away the video games, read to their child.

I speak to you not just as a President, but as a father, when I say that responsibility for our children's education must begin at home. That is not a Democratic issue or a Republican issue. That's an American issue."
Barack Obama, February 24, 2009

Obama's vision for a 21st century education begins with demanding more reform and accountability, coupled with the resources needed to carry out that reform. He will ask parents to take responsibility for their children's success; he will recruit, retain, and reward an army of new teachers to fill new successful schools that prepare our children for success in college and the workforce.

Many details of the plan are outlined below:

Expand Early Childhood Education
President Obama introduced a comprehensive "Zero to Five" plan to provide critical support to young children and their parents. By investing $10 billion per year the program will:

- Create Early Learning Challenge Grants to stimulate and help fund state "zero to five" efforts
- Quadruple the number of eligible children for Early Head Start
- Increase Head Start funding
- Work to ensure that all children have access to pre-school

- Provide affordable and high-quality child care that will promote child development and ease the burden on working families
- Create a Presidential Early Learning Council to increase collaboration and program coordination across federal, state, and local levels

Unlike other early childhood education plans, this plan will place key emphasis at early care and education for infants, which is essential for children to be ready to enter kindergarten.

K-12

From the moment our children step into a classroom, the single most important factor in determining their achievement is their teacher. Obama's plan values teachers and the central role they play in education. His plan will work to ensure competent, effective teachers in schools that are organized for success. The Obama K-12 plan will expand service scholarships to recruit and prepare teachers who commit to working in underserved districts.

To support teachers, the plan will foster ongoing improvements in teacher education, provide mentoring for beginning teachers, and create incentives for shared planning and learning time for teachers.

To retain teachers, career pathways will be developed that provide ongoing professional development and reward accomplished teachers for their expertise. The goals of this Career Ladder initiative are to eliminate teacher shortages in hard-to-staff areas and subjects, improve teacher retention rates, strengthen teacher preparation programs, improve professional development, and better utilize and reward accomplished teachers.

Reform No Child Left Behind (NCLB)

The plan will reform NCLB, which starts by funding the law. Barack Obama believes that teachers should not be forced to spend the academic year preparing students to fill in bubbles on standardized tests. His plan will improve the assessments used to track student progress to measure readiness for college and the workplace, and improve student learning in a timely, individualized manner. The plan will also improve NCLB's accountability system so that we are supporting schools that need improvement, rather than punishing them.

Support High-Quality Schools and Close Low-Performing Charter Schools

Obama's education plan will double funding for the Federal Charter School Program to support the creation of more successful charter schools. The Obama Administration will provide this expanded charter school funding only to states that:

- Agree to improve accountability for charter schools
- Allow for interventions in struggling charter schools
- Have a clear process for closing down chronically underperforming charter schools.

Obama's education plan will also prioritize support for states that help the most successful charter schools expand to serve more students.

Make Math and Science Education a National Priority

Obama will recruit math and science degree graduates to the teaching profession and will support efforts to help these teachers learn from professionals in the field. He will also work to ensure that all children have access to a strong science curriculum at all grade levels.

Reduce the High School Dropout Rate

The warning signs for high school dropouts often occur well before high school. Obama will sign into law his Success in the Middle Act to improve the education of middle school students in low-performing schools. He will also establish a competitive grant process for entities pursuing evidence-based models that have been proven to reduce dropouts.

Obama's education plan will address the dropout crisis by funding school districts so they can invest in intervention strategies in middle school—strategies such as personal academic plans, teaching teams, parent involvement, mentoring, intensive reading, math instruction, and extended learning time.

Protect Title IX

Obama supports eliminating gender discrimination in American schools. For 35 years, Title IX has been a bulwark against sex discrimination against students and employees at all levels of education. President Obama promises to fight to make sure women have equal opportunities and access from pre-kindergarten through graduate school.

Support College Outreach Programs

Support will be extended to outreach programs like GEAR UP, TRIO, and Upward Bound to encourage more young people from low-income families to consider and prepare for college.

Support College Credit Initiatives

A national "Make College A Reality" initiative will be created that has a bold goal to increase students taking AP or college-level classes nationwide by 50 percent by the year 2016. If realized, this initiative will build on Obama's bipartisan proposal in the U.S. Senate to provide grants for students seeking college level credit at community colleges.

Support English Language Learners

Support will be given to transitional bilingual education and will help Limited English Proficient students get ahead by holding schools accountable for making sure these students complete school.

Recruit Teachers

A new Teacher Service Scholarship will be created that will cover four years of undergraduate or two years of graduate teacher education, including high-quality alternative programs for mid-career recruits in exchange for teaching for at least four years in a high-need field or location.

Prepare Teachers

Obama's education plan will require all schools of education to be accredited. It will also create a voluntary national performance assessment, so that we can be sure every new educator is trained and ready to walk into the classroom and start teaching effectively. Obama will also create Teacher Residency Programs that will supply 30,000 exceptionally well-prepared recruits to high-need schools.

Retain Teachers

To support our teachers, the plan will expand mentoring programs that pair experienced teachers with new recruits. It will also provide incentives to give teachers paid common planning time so they can collaborate to share best practices.

Reward Teachers

New and innovative ways to increase teacher pay will be promoted. These will be developed with teachers, rather than imposed upon them. Districts will be able to design programs that reward, with a salary increase, accomplished educators who serve as mentors to new teachers. Districts can reward teachers who work in underserved places (like rural areas and inner cities) and if teachers consistently excel in the classroom, their work can be valued and rewarded as well.

Higher Education

Making College More Affordable

Obama's education plan will make college affordable for all Americans by creating a new American Opportunity Tax Credit. This fully refundable credit will ensure that the first $4,000 of a college education is completely free for most Americans, and will cover two-thirds the cost of tuition at the average public college or university. Recipients of this credit will be required to conduct 100 hours of public service a year, either during the school year or over the summer months.

Simplify the Application Process for Financial Aid

The plan will streamline the financial aid process by eliminating the current federal financial aid application and enabling families to apply simply by checking a box on their tax form. This box will authorize their tax information to be used and eliminate the need for a separate application.

Students with Disabilities

Obama's education plan will attempt to ensure the academic success of students with disabilities by increasing funding for and effectively enforcing the Individuals with Disabilities Education Act. It will also hold schools accountable for providing students with disabilities the services and support they need to reach their full potential. The plan will also give support to Early Intervention services for infants and toddlers, and will work to improve college opportunities for high school graduates with disabilities.

FAMILY

"...[A]t the dawn of the 21st century we also have a collective responsibility to recommit ourselves to the dream; to strengthen that safety net, put the rungs back on that ladder to the middle-class, and give every family the chance that so many of our parents and grandparents had. This responsibility is one that's been missing from Washington for far too long—a responsibility I intend to take very seriously as President."
Barack Obama, Spartanburg, SC, June 15, 2007

The American dream is increasingly out of reach for many people. Americans with incomes below $100,000 have experienced stagnating wages, declining health care coverage, erosion of pension protections, rising personal debt, and jobs disappearing as a result of global competition and rising housing costs. Further, the gap between America's richest and poorest is at its widest point in at least 25 years.

At a time when costs are rising and Americans are working harder just to keep up, President Obama will strive to provide relief for the middle class and support for working people. In addition to his health care and tax relief plans, Obama will make college affordable, reform our bankruptcy and credit card laws, protect the balance between work and family, and put a secure and dignified retirement within the reach of all Americans. President Obama has been a strong advocate for working people throughout his public life, and he will stand up to special interests and bring America together to reclaim the American dream.

Barack Obama's plan will accomplish this by offering several levels of support to working families. His plan includes:

A Tax Cut for Working Families

Fairness will be restored to the tax code and 150 million workers will receive the tax relief they need. Obama will create a new "Making Work Pay" tax credit of up to $500 per person, or $1,000 per working family. The Making Work Pay tax credit will completely eliminate income taxes for 10 million Americans.

Extend Paid Sick Days to All Workers

Half of all private sector workers have no paid sick days and the problem is worse for employees in low-paying jobs, where less than a quarter receive any paid sick days. Obama's plan supports efforts to guarantee workers seven days of paid sick leave per year, a moderate proposal that should not impose too onerous a burden on employers.

Expand the Family and Medical Leave Act (FMLA)

The FMLA covers only certain people who work for employers that have fifty or more employees. Obama's plan will expand the FMLA to cover businesses with twenty-five or more employees. It will cover more purposes including:

- Leave for workers who provide elder care
- 24 hours of leave each year for parents to participate in their children's academic activities at school
- Leave for workers who care for individuals who reside in their home for six months or more
- Leave for employees to address domestic violence and sexual assault

Encourage States to Adopt Paid Leave

President Obama's plan for families will initiate a fifty state strategy to encourage all states to adopt paid-leave systems. It will provide a $1.5 billion fund to assist states with start-up costs and to help offset the costs of paid leave for employees and employers.

Expand Afterschool Opportunities

Funding will be doubled for the main federal support for afterschool programs (the 21st Century Learning Centers program), to serve one-million more children. It will include measures to maximize performance and effectiveness across grantees nationwide.

Expand the Child and Dependent Care Tax Credit

Barack Obama believes the Child and Dependent Care Tax Credit provides too little relief to families that struggle to afford childcare expenses. He will reform the Child and Dependent Care Tax Credit by making it refundable and by allowing low-income families to receive up to a 50 percent credit for their child care expenses.

Protect Against Caregiver Discrimination

Workers with family obligations often are discriminated against in the workplace. Obama's plan will commit the government to enforcing recently-enacted Equal Employment Opportunity Commission guidelines on caregiver discrimination.

Expand Flexible Work Arrangements

The plan will address this concern by creating a program to inform businesses about the benefits and increased productivity that comes with a positive work environment. This will be accomplished through flexible work schedules, flexible work opportunities, and an increase in federal incentives for telecommuting. Obama's plan will also make the federal government a model employer in terms of adopting flexible work schedules and permitting employees to petition for flexible arrangements.

President Obama's plan will also work to strengthen families within the home. To start, the plan will re-introduce the Responsible Fatherhood and Healthy Families Act. This will do several things:

- Remove some of the government penalties on married families
- Crack down on men avoiding child support payments
- Ensure that support payments go to families instead of state bureaucracies
- Fund support services for fathers and their families
- Support domestic violence prevention efforts.

President Obama plans to sign this bill into law and continue to implement innovative measures to strengthen families. Those measures include supporting parents who have young children. **The plan** will expand programs like the successful Nurse-Family Partnership to all low-income, first-time mothers. The Nurse-Family Partnership provides home visits by trained registered nurses to low-income expectant mothers and their families.

Researchers at the Federal Reserve Bank of Minneapolis concluded that these programs produced an average of five dollars in savings for every dollar invested, and produced more than $28,000 in net savings for every high-risk family enrolled in the program. It is estimated that Obama's plan will assist approximately 570,000 first-time mothers each year.

WOMEN

"From the first moment a woman dared to speak that hope—dared to believe that the American Dream was meant for her too—ordinary women have taken on extraordinary odds to give their daughters the chance for something else; for a life more equal, more free, and filled with more opportunity than they ever had. In so many ways we have succeeded, but in so many areas we have much work left to do."
Barack Obama, Speech in Washington, DC November 10, 2005

President Obama has a long record of standing up for women. In Illinois, he passed the Equal Pay Act to give 330,000 more women protection from pay discrimination and passed another law that ensured victims of domestic violence could seek treatment without losing their jobs. In the U.S. Senate, he introduced and sponsored legislation to:

- Reduce unintended teen pregnancy
- Strengthen families by supporting fathers who are doing the right thing and cracking down on those who are not
- Guarantee workers paid sick leave
- Ensure that women are not receiving less pay than men for comparable work

Throughout his career, in the Illinois Senate, the U.S. Senate, and the White House, Obama has stood up for a woman's right to choose. Obama's plan for improving the lives of American women includes many areas of concern:

Empowering Women to Prevent HIV/AIDS

In the United States, the percentage of women diagnosed with AIDS has quadrupled over the last twenty years. Today, women account for more than one quarter of all new HIV/AIDS diagnoses. Women of color are especially hard hit: In 2004, HIV infection was the leading cause of death for African-American women between the ages of 25 and 34.

President Obama has been, and promises to be, a leader in the global fight against AIDS. In the Senate, he introduced the Microbicide Development Act, which will accelerate the development of products that empower women in the battle against AIDS. Microbicides are a class of products currently under development that women apply topically to prevent transmission of HIV and other infections.

Supporting Research into Women's Health

Heart disease is the leading cause of death among women, accounting for nearly 39 percent of all female deaths. Studies show that after a first heart attack, women are less likely than men to receive diagnostic, therapeutic, and cardiac rehabilitation procedures, and are more likely to die or to have a second heart attack. Women are also more likely than men to report having arthritis, asthma, autoimmune diseases, and depression. Health care disparities among minority and poor women are especially pervasive.

President Obama has fought to maintain funding for the Centers of Excellence in Women's Health at the Department of Health and Human Services. He also supports legislation to encourage research that will examine gender and health disparities. The same legislation would establish community outreach programs in underserved areas to help women gain access to health care and maintain healthy lifestyles.

Fighting Cancer

Ovarian cancer is the fourth-leading cause of cancer-related death among women in the United States. Because of the lack of early symptoms or a proven screening test, ovarian cancer also has the highest mortality rate of all cancers of the female reproductive system. President Obama was an original co-sponsor of Johanna's Law, a piece of legislation signed into law in January 2007, which will educate women and increase awareness of ovarian cancer. The President has also supported efforts to combat breast cancer, another leading cause of death among women. He helped pass legislation in the Illinois State Senate to expand insurance coverage for mammograms.

Reducing Health Risks Due to Mercury Pollution

More than five million women of childbearing age have high levels of toxic mercury in their blood and more than 630,000 newborns are born every year at risk. The EPA estimates that every year, more than one child in six could be at risk for developmental disorders because of mercury exposure in the mother's womb. Since the primary sources of mercury in fish come from power plant emissions that contaminate our water, regulation of utility emissions is essential to protecting the health of our children.

In the Senate, President Obama introduced two pieces of legislation to significantly reduce the amount of mercury that is deposited in oceans, lakes, and rivers, which in turn will reduce the amount of mercury in fish.

A Woman's Right to Choose

President Obama believes that abortion is a divisive issue and he respects those who disagree with him. However, he has been a consistent champion of reproductive choice and has promised to make preserving women's rights under

Roe v. Wade a priority in his Administration. He opposes any constitutional amendment to overturn the Supreme Court's decision in that case.

Preventing Unintended Pregnancy

President Obama was an original co-sponsor of legislation to expand access to contraception, health information, and preventive services to help reduce unintended pregnancies.

Introduced in January 2007, the Prevention First Act will increase funding for family planning and comprehensive sex education that teaches both abstinence and safe sex methods. The Act will also end insurance discrimination against contraception, improve awareness about emergency contraception, and provide compassionate assistance to rape victims.

Reducing Domestic Violence

One in four women will experience domestic violence in her lifetime. Family violence accounted for 11 percent of all violence between 1998 and 2002. As a member of the Senate, President Obama introduced legislation to combat domestic violence by providing $25 million a year for partnerships between domestic violence prevention organizations and Fatherhood or Marriage programs to train staff in domestic violence services, provide services to families affected by domestic violence, and to develop best practices in domestic violence prevention.

Strengthening Domestic Violence Laws

Approximately 1,400 women a year—four every day—die in the United States as a result of domestic violence. And 132,000 women report that they have been victims of a rape or attempted rape, and it is estimated that an even greater number have been raped but do not report it.

In the Senate, President Obama co-sponsored and helped reauthorize the Violence Against Women Act, legislation initially written and pushed through Congress by Vice President Biden. The law funds and helps communities, nonprofit organizations, and police combat domestic violence, sexual assault, and stalking. The reauthorized legislation establishes a sexual assault services program and provides education grants to prevent domestic violence.

Pay Equity

Despite decades of progress, women still make only 77 cents for every dollar men make. Throughout their careers, President Obama and Vice President Biden have championed the right of women to receive equal pay for equal work. In the Illinois State Senate, President Obama cosponsored and voted for the Illinois Equal Pay Act, which provided 330,000 more women protection from pay discrimination.

In the U.S. Senate, Obama joined a bipartisan group of Senators to introduce the Fair Pay Restoration Act, a bill to overturn the Supreme Court's recent 5-4 decision in Ledbetter v. Goodyear Tire & Rubber Company. The bill will restore the clear intent of Congress: that workers must have a reasonable time to file a pay discrimination claim after they become victims of discriminatory compensation.

Women-Owned Businesses

Women are majority owners of more than 28 percent of U.S. businesses, but head less than 4 percent of venture-capital-backed firms. Women business owners are more likely than white male business owners to have their loan applications denied. President Obama's Administration will encourage investing in women-owned businesses by providing more support to women business owners and reducing discrimination in lending.

Women in Math and Science

Women constitute 45 percent of the workforce in the U.S., but hold just 12 percent of science and engineering jobs in business and industry. Women also make up just 9 percent of the recipients of engineering-related bachelor's degrees. President Obama believes that every student should have equal access to education in math, science, and technology in order to compete on a global scale.

SOCIAL SECURITY & MEDICARE

"Since the New Deal, we've had a basic understanding in America. If you work hard and pay into the system, you've earned the right to a secure retirement. But even though they've held up their end of the bargain, many seniors are struggling to keep pace with costs. And as so many Americans know, their worry becomes an entire family's worry."
Barack Obama, September 18, 2007

President Obama has committed to ensuring that Social Security is solvent and viable for the American people, now and in the future. Obama promises to be honest with the American people about the long-term solvency of Social Security and the ways we can address the shortfall. Social Security benefits for current and future beneficiaries alike will be protected; the retirement age will not be raised.

Obama's plan strongly opposes the privatizing of Social Security. As part of a bipartisan plan that would be phased in over many years, he will ask those making over $250,000 to contribute a bit more to Social Security to keep it sound.

Strengthen Retirement Savings

Obama's plan for retirement will also reform corporate bankruptcy laws to protect workers and retirees. The current bankruptcy laws offer more protection to banks than to workers. The goal of Obama's plan is to protect pensions in several ways:

- Promises made to workers will be placed higher on the list of debts that companies cannot shed

- Bankruptcy courts will no longer be allowed to demand more sacrifice from workers than they do from executives
- Companies will be told that they cannot issue executive bonuses while cutting worker pensions
- Unpaid wages and benefits that workers can claim in court will be increased
- The circumstances under which retiree benefits can be reduced will be constrained

To improve retirement savings, Obama's plan will require full disclosure of company pension investments. This will ensure that all employees, who have company pensions, receive detailed annual disclosures about their pension fund's investments. This will provide retirees important resources they need to make their pension fund more secure.

The plan for savings will also:

Eliminate Income Taxes

All income taxation of seniors making less than $50,000 per year will be eliminated. This will provide an immediate tax cut, averaging $1,400, to 7 million seniors and relieve millions from the burden of filing tax returns.

Automatic Workplace Pensions

The Obama retirement security plan will automatically enroll workers in a workplace pension plan. Under their plan, employers who do not currently offer a retirement plan will be required to enroll their employees in a direct-deposit IRA account that is compatible with existing direct-deposit payroll systems. Employees may opt-out if they choose. Experts estimate that this program will increase the savings participation rate for low and middle-income workers from its current 15 percent level to around 80 percent.

Expand Savings Incentives for Working Families Obama's plan will attempt to ensure that savings incentives are fair to all workers by creating a generous savings match for low and middle-income Americans. The plan will match 50 percent of the first $1,000 of savings for families that earn less than $75,000. The savings match will be automatically deposited into designated personal accounts. Over 80 percent of these savings incentives will go to new savers.

Prevent Age Discrimination Obama's plan will fight job discrimination for aging employees by strengthening the Age Discrimination in Employment Act and empowering the Equal Employment Opportunity Commission to prevent all forms of discrimination.

Affordable Health Care

Obama's health care plan is committed to making health care accessible and affordable for all senior citizens. His health care plan addresses the needs specific to seniors in four ways:

Provide Cheaper Prescription Drugs
American seniors pay the highest prices in the world for brand-name drugs. To lower drug costs, the federal government will be allowed to negotiate for lower drug prices for the Medicare program, just as it does to lower prices for our veterans.

Protect and Strengthen Medicare
The long-term strength of the Medicare program is critically important for the health of seniors. Obama's plan will improve Medicare by reducing waste in the Medicare system—in part by eliminating subsidies to the private

insurance Medicare Advantage program—and tackle fundamental health care reform to improve the quality and efficiency of our healthcare system. The "doughnut hole" will be closed in the Medicare Part D prescription drug program.

Provide Transparency to Medicare Plans

Many seniors are enrolled in Medicare prescription drug plans that are actually more expensive for them than other available plans. Obama's plan will require companies to send Medicare beneficiaries a full list of the drugs and fees they paid the previous year to help seniors determine which plans can better reduce their out-of-pocket costs and improve their health.

Strengthen Long-Term Care Options

Obama will work to give seniors choices about their care, consistent with their needs, and not biased towards institutional care. He will work to reform the financing of long term care to protect seniors and families, and to improve the quality of elder care by training more nurses and health care workers.

To further protect and honor seniors, heating assistance will be provided. Funding will also be increased for the Low Income Home Energy Assistance Program (LIHEAP), which helps low-income citizens—many of them seniors—pay their winter heating and summer cooling bills.

Part Three

Protecting the Nation & Restoring American Values

IRAQ

"Just before America's entry into World War I, President Woodrow Wilson addressed Congress: "It is a fearful thing to lead this great peaceful people into war," he said. "...But the right is more precious than peace." Wilson's words captured two awesome responsibilities that test any Commander-in-Chief—to never hesitate to defend America, but to never go to war unless you must. War is sometimes necessary, but it has grave consequences, and the judgment to go to war can never be undone.

Five years ago today, President George W. Bush addressed the nation. Bombs had started to rain down on Baghdad. War was necessary, the President said, because the United States could not, "live at the mercy of an outlaw regime that threatens the peace with weapons of mass murder." Recalling the pain of 9/11, he said the price of inaction in Iraq was to meet the threat with "armies of fire fighters and police and doctors on the streets of our cities."

At the time the President uttered those words, there was no hard evidence that Iraq had those stockpiles of weapons of mass destruction. There was not any evidence that Iraq was responsible for the attacks of September 11, or that Iraq had operational ties to the al Qaeda terrorists who carried them out. By launching a war based on faulty premises and bad intelligence, President Bush failed Wilson's test. So did Congress when it voted to give him the authority to wage war.

Five years have gone by since that fateful decision. This war has now lasted longer than World War I, World War II, or the Civil War. Nearly four thousand Americans have given their lives. Thousands more have been wounded. Even under the best case scenarios, this war will cost American taxpayers well over a trillion dollars. And where are we for all of this sacrifice? We are less safe and less able to shape events abroad. We are divided at home, and our alliances around the world have been strained. The threats of a new century have roiled the waters of peace and stability, and yet America remains anchored in Iraq.

History will catalog the reasons why we waged a war that didn't need to be fought, but two stand out: In 2002, when the fateful decisions about Iraq were made, there was a President for whom ideology overrode pragmatism, and there were too many politicians in Washington who spent too little time reading the intelligence reports, and too much time reading public opinion. The lesson of Iraq is that when we are making decisions about matters as grave as war, we need a policy rooted in reason and facts, not ideology and politics...

...In the year since President Bush announced the surge—the bloodiest year of the war for America—the level of violence in Iraq has been reduced. Our troops—including so many from Fort Bragg and Pope Air Force Base—have done a brilliant job under difficult circumstances. Yet while we have a General who has used improved tactics to reduce violence, we still have the wrong strategy. As General Petraeus has himself acknowledged, the Iraqis are not achieving the political progress needed to end their civil war. Beyond Iraq, our military is badly overstretched, and we have neither the strategy nor resources to deal with nearly every other national security challenge we face.

This is why the judgment that matters most on Iraq—and on any decision to deploy military force—is the judgment made

THE PLAN

first. If you believe we are fighting the right war, then the problems we face are purely tactical in nature. That is what Senator McCain wants to discuss—tactics. What he and the Administration have failed to present is an overarching strategy: how the war in Iraq enhances our long-term security, or will in the future. That's why this Administration cannot answer the simple question posed by Senator John Warner in hearings last year: Are we safer because of this war? And that is why Senator McCain can argue—as he did last year—that we couldn't leave Iraq because violence was up, and then argue this year that we can't leave Iraq because violence is down.

When you have no overarching strategy, there is no clear definition of success. Success comes to be defined as the ability to maintain a flawed policy indefinitely. Here is the truth: fighting a war without end will not force the Iraqis to take responsibility for their own future. And fighting in a war without end will not make the American people safer...

...In order to end this war responsibly, I will immediately begin to remove our troops from Iraq. We can responsibly remove 1 to 2 combat brigades each month. If we start with the number of brigades we have in Iraq today, we can remove all of them 16 months. After this redeployment, we will leave enough troops in Iraq to guard our embassy and diplomats, and a counter-terrorism force to strike al Qaeda if it forms a base that the Iraqis cannot destroy. What I propose is not—and never has been—a precipitous drawdown. It is instead a detailed and prudent plan that will end a war nearly seven years after it started.

My plan to end this war will finally put pressure on Iraq's leaders to take responsibility for their future. Because we've learned that when we tell Iraq's leaders that we'll stay as long as it takes, they take as long as they want. We need to send a different message. We will help Iraq reach a meaningful accord on national reconciliation. We will engage with every country in the region—and the UN—to support the stability and territorial integrity of Iraq. And we will launch a major humanitarian initiative to support Iraq's refugees and people. But Iraqis must take responsibility for their country. It is precisely this kind of approach—an approach that puts the onus on the Iraqis, and that relies on more than just military power—that is needed to stabilize Iraq.

Let me be clear: ending this war is not going to be easy. There will be dangers involved. We will have to make tactical adjustments, listening to our commanders on the ground, to ensure that our interests in a stable Iraq are met, and to make sure that our troops are secure...."
Barack Obama, March 19, 2008

President Obama has promised to responsibly end the war in Iraq so that we can renew our military strength, dedicate more resources to the fight against the Taliban and al Qaeda in Afghanistan, and invest in our economy at home. The Obama plan will help us succeed in Iraq by transitioning to Iraqis, the control of their own country.

A Responsible, Phased Withdrawal

Immediately upon taking office, Barack Obama has promised to give his Secretary of Defense and military commanders a new mission in Iraq: ending the war. The removal of our troops, he said, will be responsible and phased, directed by military commanders on the ground, and done in consultation with the Iraqi government.

Military experts believe we can safely redeploy combat brigades from Iraq at a pace of 1 to 2 brigades a month—which would remove all of them in 16 months. That would be the summer of 2010—more than 7 years after the war began.

Under the Obama plan, a residual force will remain in Iraq and in the region to conduct targeted counter-terrorism missions against al Qaeda in Iraq and protect American diplomatic and civilian personnel. Permanent bases will not be built in Iraq, but we will continue to train and support the Iraqi security forces, as long as Iraqi leaders move toward political reconciliation and away from sectarianism.

Encourage Political Accommodation

Barack Obama believes that the U.S. must apply pressure on the Iraqi government to work toward real political accommodation. There is no military solution to Iraq's political differences. Now is the time to press Iraq's leaders to take responsibility for their future and to invest their oil revenues in their own reconstruction.

Obama's plan is to create lasting stability in Iraq. A phased withdrawal will encourage Iraqis to take the lead in securing their own country and in making political compromises. The responsible pace of redeployment, called for by the Obama plan, offers more than enough time for Iraqi leaders to get their own house in order.

As our forces redeploy, Obama promises to make sure we engage representatives from all levels of Iraqi society—in and out of government—to forge compromises on oil revenue sharing, the equitable provision of services, federalism, the status of disputed territories, new elections, aid to displaced Iraqis, and the reform of Iraqi security forces.

Surging Diplomacy

Obama will launch an aggressive diplomatic effort to reach a comprehensive agreement on the stability of Iraq and the region. This effort will include all of Iraq's neighbors— including Iran and Syria, as suggested by the bi-partisan Iraq Study Group Report. This pact will aim to secure Iraq's borders; keep neighboring countries from meddling inside Iraq; isolate al Qaeda; support reconciliation among Iraq's sectarian groups; and provide financial support for Iraq's reconstruction and development.

Prevent Humanitarian Crisis

More than five million Iraqis are refugees or are displaced inside their own country. President Obama believes that America has both a moral obligation and a responsibility for security that demands we confront Iraq's humanitarian crisis. He plans to form an international working group to address this crisis. The plan will provide at least $2 billion to expand services to Iraqi refugees in neighboring countries, and ensure that Iraqis inside their own country can find sanctuary.

Obama will also work with Iraqi authorities and the international community to hold accountable the perpetrators of potential war crimes, crimes against humanity, and genocide. He will reserve the right to intervene militarily, with our international partners, to suppress potential genocidal violence within Iraq.

The Status-of-Forces Agreement (SOFA)

Obama believes it is vital that a Status of Forces Agreement be reached so our troops have the legal protections and immunities they need. Any SOFA should be subject to Congressional review to ensure it has bipartisan support here at home.

NUCLEAR THREAT & TERRORISM

"There are still about fifty tons of highly enriched uranium—some of it poorly secured—at civilian nuclear facilities in over forty countries around the world. In the former Soviet Union, there are still about 15,000 to 16,000 nuclear weapons and stockpiles of uranium and plutonium capable of making another 40,000 weapons scattered across eleven time zones. And people have already been caught trying to smuggle nuclear materials to sell them on the black market."
Barack Obama, April 23, 2007

"As president, I will secure all loose nuclear materials around the world in my first term, seek deep cuts in global nuclear arsenals, strengthen the Nuclear Non-Proliferation Treaty, and once more seek a world without nuclear weapons...

...I also know that meeting these new threats will require a president who deploys the power of tough, principled diplomacy. It is time to present a country like Iran with a clear choice. If it abandons its nuclear program, support for terror, and threats to Israel, then Iran can rejoin the community of nations—with all the benefits that entails. If not, Iran will face deeper isolation and steeper sanctions. When we engage directly, we will be in a stronger position to rally real international support for increased pressure. We will also engender more goodwill from the Iranian people. And make no mistake—if and when we ever have to use military force against any country, we must exert the power of American diplomacy first...

...We cannot place the burden of a new national security strategy on our military alone. We must integrate our diplomatic, information, economic and military power. That is why, as soon as I take office, I will call for a National Strategy and Security Review, to help determine a 21st Century inter-agency structure to integrate the elements of our national power.

In addition, I will invest in our civilian capacity to operate alongside our troops in post-conflict zones and on humanitarian and stabilization missions. Instead of shuttering consulates in tough corners of the world, it's time to grow our Foreign Service and to expand USAID. Instead of giving up on the determination of young people to serve, it's time to double the size of our Peace Corps. Instead of letting people learn about America from enemy propaganda, it's time to recruit, train, and send out into the world an America's Voice Corps...

...We are at a defining moment in our history.

We can choose the path of unending war and unilateral action, and sap our strength and standing. We can choose the path of disengagement, and cede our leadership. Or, we can meet fear and danger head-on with hope and strength; with common purpose as a united America; and with common cause with old allies and new partners.

What we've seen these last few years is what happens when the rigid ideology and dysfunctional politics of Washington is projected abroad. An ideology that does not fit the shape of the times cannot shape events in foreign countries. A politics that is based on fear and division does not allow us to call on the world to hope, and keeps us from coming together as one people, as one nation, to write the next great chapter in the American story.

We also know that there is another face of America that we have seen these last five years. From down the road at Fort Bragg, our soldiers have gone abroad with a greater sense of common purpose than their leaders in Washington. They have learned the lessons of the 21st century's wars. And they have shown a sense of service and selflessness that represents the very best of the American character.

This must be the election when we stand up and say that we will serve them as well as they have served us. This must be the election when America comes together behind a common purpose on behalf of our security and our values. That is what we do as Americans. It's how we founded a republic based on freedom, and faced down fascism. It's how we defended democracy through a Cold War, and shined a light of hope bright enough to be seen in the darkest corners of the world.

When America leads with principle and pragmatism, hope can triumph over fear. It is time, once again, for America to lead."
Barack Obama, March 19, 2008

Barack Obama has a comprehensive strategy for terrorism and nuclear security that will reduce the danger of nuclear terrorism, prevent the spread of nuclear weapons capabilities, and strengthen the nuclear nonproliferation regime. The goals and details of his plan include:

Find, Disrupt, and Destroy Al Qaeda
Obama plans to responsibly end the war in Iraq and focus on the right battlefield in Afghanistan. He promises to

work with other nations to strengthen their capacity to eliminate shared enemies.

New Capabilities to Defeat Terrorists
He will improve the American intelligence apparatus by investing in its capacity to collect and analyze information, share information with other agencies, and carry out operations to disrupt terrorist networks.

Prepare the Military for 21st Century Threats
To ensure that our military becomes more stealth, agile, and lethal in its ability to capture or kill terrorists, Barack Obama plans to bolster our military's ability to speak different languages, navigate different cultures, and coordinate complex missions with our civilian agencies.

Win the Battle of Ideas
President Obama's goal is to defeat al Qaeda in the battle of ideas by returning to an American foreign policy consistent with America's traditional values, and working with moderates within the Islamic world to counter al Qaeda propaganda. Obama's Administration will establish a $2 billion Global Education Fund to work to eliminate the global education deficit and offer an alternative to extremist schools.

Secure Loose Nuclear Materials from Terrorists
While working to secure existing stockpiles of nuclear material, Obama promises to negotiate a verifiable global ban on the production of new nuclear weapons material. This will deny terrorists the ability to steal or buy loose nuclear materials.

President Obama believes that a global effort to secure all nuclear weapons materials at vulnerable sites within four years is the most effective way to prevent terrorists from acquiring a nuclear bomb. He plans to lead this effort and to fully implement the Lugar-Obama legislation to help our allies detect and stop the smuggling of weapons of mass destruction.

Move Toward a Nuclear Free World

Obama has a goal of a world without nuclear weapons. He promises to maintain a strong deterrent as long as nuclear weapons exist, and to take several steps down the long road toward eliminating nuclear weapons. He will stop the development of new nuclear weapons, work with Russia to take U.S. and Russian ballistic missiles off hair trigger alert, seek dramatic reductions in U.S. and Russian stockpiles of nuclear weapons and material, work to expand the U.S.-Russian ban on intermediate-range missiles so that the agreement is global.

Nuclear Non-Proliferation Treaty

Obama will crack down on nuclear proliferation by strengthening the Nuclear Non-Proliferation Treaty so that countries like North Korea and Iran, that break the rules, will automatically face strong international sanctions.

Strengthen Policing and Interdiction Efforts

Obama's plan will institutionalize the Proliferation Security Initiative (PSI), a global initiative aimed at stopping shipments of weapons of mass destruction, their delivery systems, and related materials worldwide.

Summit on Nuclear Terrorism

In 2009, Obama plans to convene a summit (and regularly thereafter) of leaders of Permanent Members of the

UN Security Council and other key countries to agree on preventing nuclear terrorism.

Iran and North Korea's Nuclear Programs

Obama believes that tough diplomacy, backed by real incentives and real pressures, is the best way to prevent Iran from acquiring nuclear weapons and to eliminate fully and verifiably North Korea's nuclear weapons program.

International Atomic Energy Agency (IAEA)

Obama's plan will ensure that the Agency gets the authority, information, people, and technology it needs to do its job.

Control Fissile Materials

Obama promises to lead a global effort to negotiate a verifiable treaty ending the production of fissile materials for weapons purposes.

Prevent Fuel from Becoming Nuclear Bombs

Obama's plan includes working with other interested governments to establish a new international nuclear energy architecture—including an international nuclear fuel bank, international nuclear fuel cycle centers, and reliable fuel supply assurances—to meet growing demands for nuclear power without contributing to proliferation.

Reduce Nuclear Stockpiles

Part of Obama's plan is to seek deep, verifiable reductions in all U.S. and Russian nuclear weapons, and to work with other nuclear powers to reduce global stockpiles.

Work with Russia to Increase Warning Time

Obama promises to work with Russia to end dangerous Cold War policies like keeping nuclear weapons ready to launch on a moment's notice, in a mutual and verifiable manner.

Appoint a Coordinator for Nuclear Security

The Obama Administration will appoint a deputy national security advisor to be in charge of coordinating all U.S. programs aimed at reducing the risk of nuclear terrorism and weapons proliferation.

Reduce Risk at Defense, State, & Energy Departments

By expanding our foreign service, and developing the capacity of our civilian aid workers to work alongside the military, Obama believes we can reduce certain levels of nuclear risk. Obama believes that thwarting terrorist networks requires international partnerships in military, intelligence, law enforcement, financial transactions, border controls, and transportation security—and his plan is to pursue those avenues.

FOREIGN POLICY

"The war in Iraq has emboldened Iran, which poses the greatest challenge to American interests in the Middle East in a generation, continuing its nuclear program and threatening our ally, Israel. Instead of the new Middle East we were promised, Hamas runs Gaza, Hizbollah flags fly from the rooftops in Sadr City, and Iran is handing out money left and right in southern Lebanon.

The war in Iraq has emboldened North Korea, which built new nuclear weapons and even tested one before the Administration finally went against its own rhetoric, and pursued diplomacy.

The war in Iraq has emboldened the Taliban, which has rebuilt its strength since we took our eye off of Afghanistan.

Above all, the war in Iraq has emboldened al Qaeda, whose recruitment has jumped and whose leadership enjoys a safe-haven in Pakistan—a thousand miles from Iraq.

The central front in the war against terror is not Iraq, and it never was. What more could America's enemies ask for than an endless war where they recruit new followers and try out new tactics on a battlefield so far from their base of operations? That is why my presidency will shift our focus. Rather than fight a war that does not need to be fought, we need to start fighting the battles that need to be won on the central front of the war against al Qaeda in Afghanistan and Pakistan.

This is the area where the 9/11 attacks were planned. This is where Osama bin Laden and his top lieutenants still hide. This is where extremism poses its greatest threat. Yet in both Afghanistan and Pakistan, we have pursued flawed strategies that are too distant from the needs of the people, and too timid in pursuit of our common enemies.

It may not dominate the evening news, but in Afghanistan, last year was the most deadly since 2001. Suicide attacks are up. Casualties are up. Corruption and drug trafficking are rampant. Neither the government nor the legal economy can meet the needs of the Afghan people.

It is not too late to prevail in Afghanistan. But we cannot prevail until we reduce our commitment in Iraq, which will allow us to do what I called for last August—providing at least two additional combat brigades to support our efforts in Afghanistan. This increased commitment in turn can be used to leverage greater assistance—with fewer restrictions—from our NATO allies. It will also allow us to invest more in training Afghan security forces, including more joint NATO operations with the Afghan Army, and a national police training plan that is effectively coordinated and resourced.

A stepped up military commitment must be backed by a long-term investment in the Afghan people. We will start with an additional $1 billion in non military assistance each year—aid that is focused on reaching ordinary Afghans. We need to improve daily life by supporting education, basic infrastructure and human services. We have to counter the opium trade by supporting alternative livelihoods for Afghan farmers. And we must call on more support from friends and allies, and better coordination under a strong international coordinator.

To succeed in Afghanistan, we also need to fundamentally rethink our Pakistan policy. For years, we have supported stability over democracy in Pakistan, and gotten neither. The core leadership of al Qaeda has a safe-haven in Pakistan. The Taliban are able to strike inside Afghanistan and then return to the mountains of the Pakistani border. Throughout Pakistan, domestic unrest has been rising. The full democratic aspirations of the Pakistani people have been too long denied. A child growing up in Pakistan, more often than not, is taught to see America as a source of hate—not hope....

...The choice is not between Musharraf and Islamic extremists. As the recent legislative elections showed, there is a moderate majority of Pakistanis, and they are the people we need on our side to win the war against al Qaeda. That is why we should dramatically increase our support for the Pakistani people—for education, economic development, and democratic institutions. That child in Pakistan must know that we want a better life for him, that America is on his side, and that his interest in opportunity is our interest as well. That's the promise that America must stand for.

And for his sake and ours, we cannot tolerate a sanctuary for terrorists who threaten America's homeland and Pakistan's stability. If we have actionable intelligence about high-level al Qaeda targets in Pakistan's border region, we must act if Pakistan will not or cannot. Senator Clinton, Senator McCain, and President Bush have all distorted and derided this position, suggesting that I would invade or bomb Pakistan. This is politics, pure and simple.

My position, in fact, is the same pragmatic policy that all three of them have belatedly—if tacitly—acknowledged is one we should pursue. Indeed, it was months after I called for this policy that a top al Qaeda leader was taken out in Pakistan by an American aircraft. And remember that the same three individuals who now criticize me for supporting a targeted strike on the terrorists who carried out the 9/11 attacks, are the same three individuals that supported an invasion of Iraq—a country that had nothing to do with 9/11.

It is precisely this kind of political point-scoring that has opened up the security gap in this country. We have a security gap when candidates say they will follow Osama bin Laden to the gates of hell, but refuse to follow him where he actually goes....

...What we need is a pragmatic strategy that focuses on fighting our real enemies, rebuilding alliances, and renewing our engagement with the world's people.

In addition to freeing up resources to take the fight to al Qaeda, ending the war in Iraq will allow us to more effectively confront other threats in the world—threats that cannot be conquered with an occupying army or dispatched with a single decision in the middle of the night. What lies in the heart of a child in Pakistan matters as much as the airplanes we sell her government.

What's in the head of a scientist from Russia can be as lethal as a plutonium reactor in Yongbyon. What's whispered in refugee camps in Chad can be as dangerous as a dictator's bluster. These are the neglected landscapes of the 21st century, where technology and extremism empower individuals just as they give governments the ability to repress them; where the ancient divides of region and religion wash into the swift currents of globalization.

Without American leadership, these threats will fester. With strong American leadership, we can shape them into opportunities to protect our common security and advance our common humanity—for it has always been the genius of American leadership to find opportunity embedded in adversity; to focus on a source of fear, and confront it with hope."
Barack Obama, March 19, 2008

President Obama has promised to renew America's security and standing in the world through a new era of American leadership. The policy will end the war in Iraq responsibly, finish the fight against the Taliban and al Qaeda in Afghanistan, secure nuclear weapons and loose nuclear materials from terrorists, and renew American diplomacy to support strong alliances and to seek a lasting peace in the Israeli-Palestinian conflict.

Pakistan
Obama's policy will increase nonmilitary aid to Pakistan and hold them accountable for security in the border region with Afghanistan.

Afghanistan
Obama's foreign policy strategy will refocus American resources on the greatest threat to our security—the resurgence of al Qaeda, and the Taliban in Afghanistan and Pakistan. It will increase our troop levels in Afghanistan, press our allies in NATO to do the same, and dedicate more resources to revitalize Afghanistan's economic development. Obama will demand the Afghan government do more,

including cracking down on corruption and the illicit opium trade.

Iran

Barack Obama supports tough and direct diplomacy with Iran without preconditions. He believes that now is the time to use the power of American diplomacy to pressure Iran to stop their illicit nuclear program, support for terrorism, and threats toward Israel.

Obama plans to offer the Iranian regime a choice: If Iran abandons its nuclear program and support for terrorism, we will offer incentives like membership in the World Trade Organization, economic investments, and a move toward normal diplomatic relations. If Iran continues its troubling behavior, we will step up our economic pressure and political isolation.

In carrying out this diplomacy, Obama plans to coordinate closely with our allies and proceed with careful preparation. Obama believes that seeking this kind of comprehensive settlement with Iran is our best way to make progress.

Israel

Barack Obama strongly supports the U.S.-Israel relationship, and believes that our first and incontrovertible commitment in the Middle East must be to the security of Israel—America's strongest ally in the region. He supports this closeness and has stated that the United States will never distance itself from Israel.

Obama supports Israel's right to self defense. During the July 2006 Lebanon war, Barack Obama stood up strongly for Israel's right to defend itself from Hezbollah's raids and rocket attacks, cosponsoring a Senate resolution against Iran and Syria's involvement in the war, and insisting that Israel should not be pressured into a ceasefire that did not deal with the threat of Hezbollah missiles.

Israel will continue to receive American support and assistance. Barack Obama has consistently supported foreign assistance to Israel. He defends and supports the annual foreign aid package that involves both military and economic assistance to Israel and has advocated increased foreign aid budgets to ensure that these funding priorities are met. He has called for continuing U.S. cooperation with Israel in the development of missile defense systems.

Obama promises to make progress on the Israeli-Palestinian conflict a key diplomatic priority from day one. He will make a sustained push—working with Israelis and Palestinians—to achieve the goal of two states: a Jewish state in Israel and a Palestinian state, living side by side in peace and security.

Darfur

President Obama has been a leading voice in Washington, urging the end of genocide in Sudan. He worked with Senator Sam Brownback (R-KS) on the Darfur Peace and Accountability Act, a version of which was signed into law. The President has traveled to the United Nations to meet with Sudanese officials and visited refugee camps on the Chad-Sudan border to raise international awareness of the ongoing humanitarian disaster there. He also worked with Senator Harry Reid (D-NV) to secure $20 million for the African Union peacekeeping mission.

Renewing American Diplomacy

Obama's foreign policy will attempt to rebuild our alliances to meet the common challenges of the 21st century. Obama believes that America is strongest when we act alongside strong partners. He believes that now is the time for a new era of international cooperation that strengthens old partnerships and builds new ones.

Talk to our Foes and Friends

President Obama will pursue tough, direct diplomacy without preconditions with all nations, friend and foe. He promises to do the careful preparation necessary, but will signal that America is ready to come to the table and is willing to lead.

Obama believes that if America is willing to come to the table, the world will be more willing to rally behind American leadership to deal with challenges like confronting terrorism as well as Iran and North Korea's nuclear programs.

Restore American Influence and Values

To make diplomacy a priority, Obama plans to move U.S. consulates abroad from undemanding positions into areas where they can better serve American interests. He aims to open consulates in the tough and hopeless corners of the world, expand our foreign service, and develop the capacity of our civilian aid workers to work alongside the military.

Fight Global Poverty

Obama embraces the Millennium Development Goal of cutting extreme poverty and hunger around the world in half by 2015. He will double our foreign assistance to achieve that goal. This will help the world's weakest states build healthy and educated communities, reduce poverty, develop markets, and generate wealth.

Seek New Partnerships in Asia

Obama plans to forge a more effective framework in Asia that goes beyond bilateral agreements, occasional summits, and ad hoc arrangements, such as the six-party talks on North Korea. He wants to maintain strong ties with allies like Japan, South Korea, and Australia; work to build an infrastructure with countries in East Asia that can promote stability and prosperity; and work to ensure that China plays by international rules.

HOMELAND SECURITY

"We are here to do the work that ensures no other family members have to lose a loved one to a terrorist who turns a plane into a missile, a terrorist who straps a bomb around her waist and climbs aboard a bus, a terrorist who figures out how to set off a dirty bomb in one of our cities. This is why we are here: to make our country safer and make sure the nearly 3,000 who were taken from us did not die in vain; that their legacy will be a more safe and secure Nation."
Barack Obama, Speech in the U.S. Senate, March 6, 2007

Barack Obama's strategy for securing the homeland against 21st century threats is focused on planning for emergencies and investing in strong response and recovery capabilities. Obama has promised to strengthen our homeland against all hazards—including natural or accidental disasters—and ensure that the federal government works with states, localities, and the private sector as a true partner in prevention, mitigation, and response.

Bio-Security

Biological weapons pose a serious and increasing national security risk. Barack Obama promises to deter bio-terror attacks and mitigate consequences in four ways:

Prevent Bio-terror Attacks
The Obama Administration will strengthen U.S. intelligence collection overseas to identify and interdict would-be bioterrorists before they strike.

Mitigate the Consequences of Bio-terror Attacks

Obama promises to ensure that decision-makers have the information and communication tools they need to manage disease outbreaks by linking health care providers, hospitals, and public health agencies. A well-planned, well-rehearsed, and rapidly executed epidemic response can dramatically diminish the consequences of biological attacks.

New Medicines, Vaccines, and Production Capabilities

Obama plans to build on America's unparalleled talent to create new drugs, vaccines, and diagnostic tests and to manufacture them more quickly and efficiently.

Diminish Impact of Infectious Disease Epidemics

President Obama's plan will promote international efforts to develop new diagnostics, vaccines, and medicines that will be available and affordable in all parts of the world. This will reduce the likelihood of epidemics that begin in one area of the world and quickly spread throughout the planet.

Protect Our Information Networks

Barack Obama—working with private industry, the research community, and our citizens—promises to lead an effort to build a trustworthy and accountable cyber infrastructure that is resilient, protects America's competitive advantage, and advances our national and homeland security. He will execute this plan in several ways:

Strengthen Cyber Security

Declare the cyber infrastructure a strategic asset and establish the position of national cyber advisor, who will report directly to the president and who will be responsible for coordinating federal agency efforts and development of national cyber policy.

Initiate a Safe Computing R&D Effort

Support an initiative to develop next-generation secure computers and networking for national security applications. Work with industry and academia to develop and deploy a new generation of secure hardware and software for our critical cyber infrastructure.

Protect Our IT Infrastructure

Because IT infrastructure is critical for the security not only of individuals, but of the country as a whole, Obama will work with the private sector to establish tough new standards for cyber security and physical resilience.

Prevent Corporate Cyber-Espionage

Work with industry to develop the systems necessary to protect our nation's trade secrets as well as our research and development. Innovations in software, engineering, pharmaceuticals, and other fields are being stolen online from U.S. businesses at an alarming rate. This is a threat to our economic security as well as our military.

Develop a Cyber Crime Strategy

Shut down the mechanisms used to transmit criminal profits by shutting down untraceable Internet payment schemes. Initiate a grant and training program to provide federal, state, and local law enforcement agencies the tools they need to detect and prosecute cyber crime.

Mandate Standards for Securing Personal Data

Partner with businesses and citizens to secure personal data stored on government and private systems. Institute a common standard for securing such data across industries and protect the rights of individuals in the information age. Require companies to disclose personal information data breaches.

Intelligence Capacity and Civil Liberties

Barack Obama's plan will improve our intelligence system by creating a senior position to coordinate domestic intelligence gathering, establishing a grant program to support thousands more state and local level intelligence analysts, and increasing our capacity to share intelligence across all levels of government.

Authority to Privacy & Civil Liberties Board

Obama's plan supports the efforts to strengthen the Privacy and Civil Liberties Board with subpoena powers and reporting responsibilities. His plan will give the Board a robust mandate designed to protect American civil liberties and demand transparency from the Board to ensure accountability.

Strengthen Institutions to Fight Terrorism

A Shared Security Partnership Program will be established overseas to invest $5 billion over three years to improve cooperation between U.S. and foreign intelligence and law enforcement agencies.

Protect Americans from Attacks Disasters

President Obama will keep the broken promises made by President Bush to rebuild New Orleans and the Gulf Coast. He will take steps to ensure that the federal government will never again allow such catastrophic failures in emergency planning and response to occur.

President Obama swiftly responded to Hurricane Katrina. Citing the Bush Administration's "unconscionable ineptitude" in responding to Hurricane Katrina, then-Senator Obama introduced legislation requiring disaster planners to take into account the specific needs of low-income victims.

President Obama has made clear that he understands the importance of emergency planning and preparedness. His plan for protecting Americans from, or in the event of, a natural or intentional disaster are outlined below.

Allocate Funds Based on Risk

Allocate our homeland security dollars according to risk, not as pork-barrel spending or a form of general revenue sharing. Eliminate waste, fraud, and abuse that cost the nation billions of Department of Homeland Security dollars.

Emergency Response Plans

Further improve coordination between all levels of government, create better evacuation plan guidelines, ensure prompt federal assistance to emergency zones, and increase medical surge capacity.

Support First Responders

Increase federal resources and logistic support to local emergency planning efforts, so that if a disaster strikes, victims will receive the care and attendance they require.

Interoperable Communications Systems

Support efforts to provide greater technical assistance to local and state first responders and dramatically increase funding for reliable, interoperable communications systems. Appoint a National Chief Technology Officer to ensure that the current non-interoperable plans at the federal, state, and local levels are combined, funded, implemented, and effective.

State and Local Governments and the Private Sector
Make the federal government a better partner to states and localities, one that listens to local concerns and considers local priorities. Reach out to the private sector to leverage its expertise and assets to protect our homeland security.

Protect Critical Infrastructure

National Infrastructure Protection Plan
Develop an effective critical infrastructure protection and resiliency plan for the nation and work with the private sector to ensure that targets are protected against all hazards.

Secure our Chemical Plants
Work with all stakeholders to enact permanent federal chemical plant security regulations.

Improve Airline Security
Redouble our efforts to adequately address the threats our nation continues to face from airplane-based terrorism.

Monitor our Ports
Redouble our efforts to develop technology that can detect radiation and work with the maritime transportation industry to deploy this technology to maximize security without causing economic disruption.

Safeguard Public Transportation

Work to protect the public transportation systems Americans use to get to work, school, and beyond every day.

Improve Border Security

Support the virtual and physical infrastructure and manpower necessary to secure our borders and keep our nation safe.

Modernize America's Aging Infrastructure

Build-in Security

Ensure that security is considered and built into the design of new infrastructure, so that our critical assets are protected from the start and more resilient to naturally occurring and deliberate threats throughout their life-cycles.

National Infrastructure Reinvestment Bank

Address the infrastructure challenge by creating a National Infrastructure Reinvestment Bank of $60 billion over 10 years, to expand and enhance, not supplant, existing federal transportation investments. This independent entity will be directed to invest in our nation's most challenging transportation infrastructure needs, without the influence of special interests.

Critical Infrastructure Projects

Invest in our nation's most pressing short and long-term infrastructure needs, including modernizing our electrical grid and upgrading our highway, rail, ports, water, and aviation infrastructure. Establish a Grid Modernization Commission to facilitate adoption of Smart Grid practices to improve the efficiency and security of our electricity grid.

DEFENSE

"Our country's greatest military asset is the men and women who wear the uniform of the United States. When we do send our men and women into harm's way, we must also clearly define the mission, prescribe concrete political and military objectives, seek out the advice of our military commanders, evaluate the intelligence, plan accordingly, and ensure that our troops have the resources, support, and equipment they need to protect themselves and fulfill their mission."
Barack Obama, Chicago Foreign Affairs Council April 23, 2007

"As Commander in Chief, I will begin by giving a military overstretched by Iraq the support it needs. It is time to reduce the strain on our troops by completing the effort to increase our ground forces by 65,000 soldiers and 27,000 Marines, while ensuring the quality of our troops. In an age marked by technology, it is the people of our military—our Soldiers, Sailors, Airmen, Marines, and Coast Guardsmen—who bear the responsibility for complex missions. That is why we need to ensure adequate training and time home between deployments. That is why we need to expand our Special Forces. And that is why we must increase investments in capabilities like civil affairs and training foreign militaries."
Barack Obama, March 19, 2008

President Obama's plan will invest in a 21st century military to maintain our conventional advantage while increasing our capacity to defeat the threats of tomorrow. It will ensure our troops have the training, equipment, and support that they need when they are deployed. The details of his plan are described below.

Rebuild the Military for 21st Century Needs

Obama believes that we must build up our special operations forces, civil affairs, information operations, and other units and capabilities that remain in chronic short supply. He plans to invest in foreign language training, cultural awareness, human intelligence, and other needed counterinsurgency and stabilization skill sets. Further, he promises to create a more robust capacity to train, equip, and advise foreign security forces so that local allies are better prepared to confront mutual threats.

Meet Military Needs on the Ground

Obama supports plans to increase the size of the Army by 65,000 soldiers and the Marine Corps by 27,000 Marines. Increasing our end-strength will help units retrain and re-equip properly between deployments and decrease the strain on military families.

Leadership from the Top

President Obama's goal is to inspire a new generation of Americans to serve their country, whether it be in local communities in such roles as teachers or first responders, or serving in the military to keep our nation free and safe.

Lighten the Burden on Troops and Families

The Obama Administration will create a Military Families Advisory Board to provide a conduit for military families' concerns to be brought to the attention of senior policymakers and the public. It will end the stop-loss policy and establish predictability in deployments so that active duty and reserves know what they can and must expect.

Fully Equip Our Troops

Barack Obama promises to get essential equipment to our soldiers, sailors, airmen, and Marines before lives are lost.

Review Weapons Programs

Obama believes we must rebalance our capabilities to ensure that our forces can succeed in both conventional wars as well as stabilization and counter-insurgency operations. Obama has committed to a review of each major defense program in light of current needs, gaps in the field, and likely future threat scenarios in the post-9/11 world.

Preserve Global Reach in the Air

Obama wants to preserve our unparalleled airpower capabilities to deter and defeat any conventional competitors, swiftly respond to crises across the globe, and support our ground forces. We need greater investment in advanced technology ranging from the revolutionary, like Unmanned Aerial Vehicles and electronic warfare capabilities, to essential systems like the C-17 cargo and KC-X air refueling aircraft, which provide the backbone of our ability to extend global power.

Maintain Power Projection at Sea

President Obama promises to recapitalize our naval forces by replacing aging ships and modernizing existing platforms, while adapting them to the 21st century. He will add to the Maritime Pre-Positioning Force Squadrons to support operations ashore and invest in smaller, more capable ships, providing the agility to operate close to shore and the reach to rapidly deploy Marines to areas of crisis.

National Missile Defense

The Obama Administration will support missile defense, but promises to ensure that it is developed in a way that is pragmatic and cost-effective. Most importantly, Obama believes the development of such a system cannot divert resources from other national security priorities until we are positive the technology will protect the American public.

Ensure Freedom of Space

The Obama Administration will strive to restore American leadership on space issues, seeking a worldwide ban on weapons that interfere with military and commercial satellites. He will thoroughly assess possible threats to U.S. space assets and the best options, military and diplomatic, for countering them.

He hopes to achieve this by establishing contingency plans that will ensure U.S. forces can maintain, or duplicate, access to information from space assets and by accelerating programs that harden U.S. satellites against attack.

Modernize the National Guard and Reserves

The National Guard will receive the equipment it needs for foreign and domestic emergencies as well as time to restore and refit before deploying. Obama plans to make the head of the National Guard a member of the Joint Chiefs of Staff, to ensure concerns of our citizen soldiers reach the level they mandate. He will ensure that reservists and Guard members are treated fairly when it comes to employment, health, and education benefits.

Integrate Military and Civilian Efforts

The capacity of each non-Pentagon agency will be built up in order to deploy personnel and area experts where they are needed This will aid the U.S. in moving soldiers, sailors, airmen and Marines out of civilian roles and into their intended service positions.

Civilian Assistance Corps (CAC)

Obama's plan will create a national CAC of 25,000 personnel. This corps of civilian volunteers with special skill sets (doctors, lawyers, engineers, city planners, agriculture specialists, police, etc.) will be organized to provide each federal agency with a pool of volunteer experts willing to deploy in times of need at home and abroad.

Engage Allies to Common Security Challenges

For common security concerns like Afghanistan, homeland security, and counterterrorism, America's traditional alliances, such as NATO, must be transformed and strengthened. President Obama's plan will renew alliances and ensure our allies contribute their fair share to our mutual security.

Help Our Partners and Allies in Need

The Obama Administration will expand humanitarian activities that build friendships and attract allies at the regional and local level (such as during the response to the tsunami in Southeast Asia) and win the hearts and minds in the process.

Create Transparency for Military Contractors

Rather than continually handing off governmental jobs to well-connected companies, Obama's plan will require the Pentagon and State Department to develop a strategy for determining when contracting makes sense. It will create the transparency and accountability needed for good governance, and establish the legal status of contractor personnel, making possible prosecution of any abuses committed by private military contractors.

Restore Commonsense to Contracting

To reduce wasteful spending, the Obama Administration promises to reduce the corruption and cost overruns that have become so common in defense contracting. This includes launching a program of acquisition reform and management, which will end the common practice of no-bid contracting.

Obama's plan aims to end the abuse of supplemental budgets by creating a system of oversight for war funds as stringent as in the regular budget. It will restore the government's ability to manage contracts by rebuilding our contract officer corps. It will order the Justice Department to prioritize prosecutions that will punish and deter fraud, waste, and abuse.

Part Four

Improving Our Communities

Veterans

Civil Rights

Poverty

Rural Policy

Urban Policy

Community Service

Disabilities

Immigration

VETERANS

"Keeping faith with those who serve must always be a core American value and a cornerstone of American patriotism. Because America's commitment to its servicemen and women begins at enlistment, and it must never end...

...To keep our sacred trust, I will improve mental health screening and treatment at all levels: from enlistment, to deployment, to reentry into civilian life. No service-member should be kicked out of the military because they are struggling with untreated PTSD. No veteran should have to fill out a 23-page claim to get care, or wait months—even years— to get an appointment at the VA. We need more mental health professionals, more training to recognize signs and to reject the stigma of seeking care. And to treat a signature wound of these wars, we need clear standards of care for Traumatic Brain Injury.

We also need to provide more services to our military families. Let me thank the VFW for helping families with everything from repairs and errands to calling cards that bring a loved one nearer. Efforts like Operation Uplink make a huge difference. You are filling in some of the painful spaces in peoples' lives. And anyone who has visited our military hospitals has seen wonderful spouses who don't see visiting hours as part-time. That's why I passed a bill to provide family members with a year of job protection, so they never have to face a choice between caring for a loved one and keeping a job...

...But we know that the sacred trust cannot expire when the uniform comes off. When we fail to keep faith with our veterans, the bond between our nation and our nation's heroes becomes frayed. When a veteran is denied care, we are all dishonored. It's not enough to lay a wreath on Memorial Day, or to pay tribute to our veterans in speeches. A proud and grateful nation owes more than ceremonial gestures and kind words.

Caring for those who serve—and for their families—is a fundamental responsibility of the Commander-in-Chief. It is not a separate cost. It is a cost of war. It is something I've fought for as a member of the Senate Committee on Veterans' Affairs. And it is something I will fight for as President of the United States...

...It's time to fully fund the VA medical center. No more delays. It's time to pass on-time VA budgets each and every year. No more means testing. It's time to allow all veterans back into the VA. I will immediately reverse a policy that led the VA to turn away nearly 1 million middle and low-income veterans since 2003.

The VA will also be at the cutting edge of my plan for universal health care, with better preventive care, more research and specialty treatment, and more Vet Centers, particularly in rural areas.

I will revamp an overburdened benefits system. The VFW has done a remarkable job helping more than 120,000 veterans a year navigate the broken VBA bureaucracy, but you shouldn't have to do it alone. I will hire additional workers, and create an electronic system that is fully linked up to military records and the VA's health network.

THE PLAN

One of the most admired principles of the U.S. military is that no one gets left behind. Yet too often America does not keep faith with this principle. On any given night, more than 200,000 veterans are homeless. We're already hearing about hundreds of homeless Iraq War vets. That's not right. That's not keeping our sacred trust. We must not leave these men and women behind. My principle will be simple: zero tolerance. Zero tolerance for veterans sleeping on the streets. I've fought for this in the Senate, and as President I'll expand housing vouchers, and I'll launch a new supportive services housing program to prevent at-risk veterans and their families from sliding into homelessness.

I'll also keep faith with America's veterans by helping them achieve their dreams. We need a G.I. Bill for the 21st century. An Obama Administration will expand access to education for our veterans, and increase benefits to keep pace with rising costs. All who wear the uniform of the United States are entitled to the same opportunity that my grandfather had under the G.I. Bill.

And our sacred trust does not end when a service-member dies. The graves of our veterans are hallowed ground. When men and women who die in service to this country are laid to rest, there must be no protests near the funerals. It's wrong and it needs to stop...

...The Americans who fight today believe in this country deeply. And no matter how many you meet, or how many stories of heroism you hear, every encounter reminds you that they are truly special. That through their service, they are living out the ideals that stir so many of us as Americans— pride, duty, and sacrifice.

Some of the most inspiring are those you meet at places like Walter Reed Medical Center. Young men and women who may have lost a limb or even their ability to take care of themselves, but will never lose the pride they feel for serving their country. They're not interested in self-pity, but yearn to move forward with their lives. And it's this classically American optimism that makes you realize the quality of person we have serving in the United States Armed Forces.

I know all of us don't agree on everything. I have heard those of you who disagree with me...And I will be clear that whatever disagreements we have on policy, there will be no daylight between us when it comes to honoring these men and women who serve, and keeping faith with our veterans. This is not a partisan issue. This is a moral obligation. This must be a beachhead for bringing our country together.

Some like to say this country is divided. But that is not how I choose to see it. I see a country that all of us love—a country that my grandfather served, and that my father crossed an ocean to reach. I see values that all of us share—values of liberty, equality, and service to a common good and a greater good. I see a flag that we fly with pride. I see an America that is the strongest nation in the history of the world—not just because of our arms, but because of the strength of our values, and of the men and women who serve." *Barack Obama, August 21, 2007*

As a member of the Senate Committee on Veterans' Affairs, Barack Obama fought to end benefit disparities, bring homeless veterans off the street, strengthen mental health care, add billions of dollars in additional Department of Veterans Affairs funding, and reform a system that often places barriers between veterans and the benefits they have earned.

A Sacred Trust

An important focus of Obama's plan for veterans is to ensure that we honor the sacred trust to care for them. By creating a 21st Century Department of Veterans' Affairs that provides the care and benefits our nation's veterans deserve, we can once again, treat our veterans with the respect and dignity they have earned.

The plan will:

Allow All Veterans Back into the VA: Reverse the 2003 ban on enrolling modest-income veterans, which has denied care to a million veterans.

Strengthen VA Care: Make the VA a leader of national health care reform so that veterans get the best care possible. Improve care for poly-trauma vision impairment, prosthetics, spinal cord injury, aging, and women's health.

Combat Homelessness among Our Nation's Veterans: Establish a national "zero tolerance" policy for veterans falling into homelessness by expanding proven programs and launching innovative services to prevent veterans from becoming homeless.

Fight Employment Discrimination: Crack down on employers who commit job discrimination against guardsmen and reservists.

Help for Returning Service Members

To improve the quality of health care for veterans, Obama's plan will rebuild the VA's broken benefits system and combat homelessness among veterans.

Ensure a Seamless Transition: Demand that the military and the VA coordinate to provide veterans with a seamless transition from active duty to civilian life.

Fully Fund VA Medical Care: Fully fund the VA so it has all the resources it needs to serve the veterans who need assistance. Establish a world-class VA Planning Division to avoid future budget shortfalls.

Improve the Bureaucracy: Hire additional claims workers and improve training and accountability so that VA benefit decisions are rated fairly and consistently. Transform the paper benefit claims process to an electronic one to reduce errors and improve timeliness.

Improve Mental Health Treatment: Recruit more health professionals, improve screening, offer more support to families, and improve the fairness of Post Traumatic Stress Disorder (PTSD) benefits.

Improve Care for Traumatic Brain Injury: Establish standards of care for Traumatic Brain Injury, the signature injury of the Iraq war.

Expand Vet Centers: Expand and strengthen Vet Centers to provide more counseling for vets and their families.

Caring for Women Veterans

There are 1.7 million women veterans, a number that is increasing every day. The Department of Veterans Affairs (VA) that was built to care for World War II veterans is not ready to handle the influx of female veterans from Iraq and Afghanistan.

As a member of the Senate Veterans Affairs Committee, then Senator Obama introduced legislation to force the Pentagon and VA to better track the newest generation of veterans—including the number of women veterans—so that the VA can better plan their care. President Obama also introduced legislation to fight homelessness among veterans, with a special focus on treating women who may have been victims of sexual trauma.

Along with Senator Claire McCaskill, President Obama co-sponsored legislation to provide funding for additional caseworkers and mental health counselors, a women's mental health treatment program, and a comprehensive mental health study of returning soldiers. The President will fight to ensure that women can get the care they deserve at the VA.

CIVIL RIGHTS

"The teenagers and college students who left their homes to march in the streets of Birmingham and Montgomery; the mothers who walked instead of taking the bus after a long day of doing somebody else's laundry and cleaning somebody else's kitchen—they didn't brave fire hoses and Billy clubs so that their grandchildren and their great-grandchildren would still wonder at the beginning of the 21st century whether their vote would be counted; whether their civil rights would be protected by their government; whether justice would be equal and opportunity would be theirs.... We have more work to do."
Barack Obama, Howard University, September 28, 2007

Whether promoting economic opportunity, working to improve our nation's education and health system, or protecting the right to vote, President Obama has been a powerful advocate for our civil rights.

During his term(s) in office, Obama plans to address several areas of America's civil rights:

Combat Employment Discrimination

President Obama wants to overturn the Supreme Court's recent ruling that curtails the ability of racial minorities and women to challenge pay discrimination. He also hopes to pass the Fair Pay Act, to ensure that women receive equal pay for equal work, and the Employment Non-Discrimination Act, to prohibit discrimination based on sexual orientation or gender identity or expression.

Expand Hate Crimes Statutes

President Obama will strengthen federal hate crimes legislation, expand hate crimes protection by passing the Matthew Shepard Act, and reinvigorate enforcement at the Department of Justice's Criminal Section.

End Deceptive Voting Practices

President Obama hopes to sign into law legislation that establishes harsh penalties for those who have engaged in voter fraud and provides voters, who have been misinformed, with accurate and full information so they can vote.

End Racial Profiling

Racial profiling by federal law enforcement agencies will be banned and federal incentives will be provided to state and local police departments to prohibit the practice.

Expand Drug Courts and End Sentencing Disparities

President Obama's plan will give first-time, non-violent offenders a chance to serve their sentence, where appropriate, in the type of drug rehabilitation programs that have proven to work better than a prison term in changing bad behavior.

He also believes the disparity between sentencing crack and powder-based cocaine is wrong and should be eliminated.

Support for the LGBT Community

"While we have come a long way since the Stonewall riots in 1969, we still have a lot of work to do. Too often, the issue of LGBT rights is exploited by those seeking to divide us. But at its core, this issue is about who we are as Americans. It's about whether this nation is going to live up to its founding

promise of equality by treating all its citizens with dignity and respect."
Barack Obama, June 1, 2007

Expand Hate Crimes Statutes

In 2004, crimes against LGBT Americans constituted the third-highest category of hate crime reported and made up more than 15 percent of such crimes. President Obama cosponsored legislation that would expand federal jurisdiction to include violent hate crimes perpetrated because of race, color, religion, national origin, sexual orientation, gender identity, or physical disability.

Fight Workplace Discrimination

President Obama supports the Employment Non-Discrimination Act, and believes that our anti-discrimination employment laws should be expanded to include sexual orientation and gender identity. While an increasing number of employers have extended benefits to their employees' domestic partners, discrimination based on sexual orientation in the workplace occurs with no federal legal remedy. The President also sponsored legislation in the Illinois State Senate that would ban employment discrimination on the basis of sexual orientation.

Support Civil Unions and Rights for LGBT Couples

President Obama supports full civil unions that give same-sex couples legal rights and privileges equal to those of married couples. Obama also believes we need to repeal the Defense of Marriage Act and enact legislation that would ensure that the 1,100+ federal legal rights and benefits currently provided on the basis of marital status are extended to same-sex couples in civil unions and other legally-recognized unions. These rights and benefits include the right to assist a loved one in times of emergency, the right to equal health insurance and other employment benefits, and property rights.

Oppose a Constitutional Ban on Same-Sex Marriage

President Obama voted against the Federal Marriage Amendment in 2006 which would have defined marriage as "between a man and a woman" and prevented judicial extension of marriage-like rights to same-sex or other unmarried couples.

Repeal Don't Ask-Don't Tell

President Obama agrees with former Chairman of the Joint Chiefs of Staff, John Shalikashvili, and other military experts, that we need to repeal the military's "don't ask, don't tell" policy. The key test for military service should be patriotism, a sense of duty, and a willingness to serve. Discrimination should be prohibited.

The U.S. government has spent millions of dollars replacing troops kicked out of the military because of their sexual orientation. Additionally, more than 300 language experts have been fired under this policy, including more than fifty who are fluent in Arabic. President Obama has promised to work with military leaders to repeal the current policy and ensure it helps accomplish our national defense goals.

Expand Adoption Rights

President Obama believes that we must ensure adoption rights for all couples and individuals, regardless of their sexual orientation. He thinks that a child will benefit from a healthy and loving home, whether the parents are gay or not.

POVERTY

"I'm in this race for the same reason that I fought for jobs for the jobless and hope for the hopeless on the streets of Chicago; for the same reason I fought for justice and equality as a civil rights lawyer; for the same reason that I fought for Illinois families for over a decade... That's why I'm running...to keep the American Dream alive for those who still hunger for opportunity, who still thirst for equality."
Barack Obama, Speech in Des Moines, IA, November 10, 2007

President Obama has been a lifelong advocate for the poor. As a young college graduate, he rejected the high salaries of corporate America and moved to the South Side of Chicago to work as a community organizer. As an organizer, Obama worked with churches, Chicago residents, and local government to set up job training programs for the unemployed and after-school programs for kids.

Barack Obama will lead a new federal approach to America's high-poverty areas, an approach that will facilitate the economic integration of families and communities with efforts to support the current low-income residents of those areas. The details of his plan are explained below:

Help Americans Climb the Job Ladder

Obama's plan will invest $1 billion, over five years, in transitional jobs and career pathway programs that implement proven methods of helping low-income Americans succeed in the workforce.

Create a Green Jobs Corps

Obama will create a program to directly engage disadvantaged youth in energy efficiency opportunities to strengthen their communities, while also providing them with practical skills in this important high-growth career field.

Improve Transportation Access to Jobs

President Obama will work to ensure that low-income Americans have transportation access to jobs. Obama will double funding for the federal Jobs Access and Reverse Commute program to ensure that additional federal public transportation dollars flow to the highest-need communities and that urban planning initiatives take this aspect of transportation policy into account.

Raise the Minimum Wage

Barack Obama believes that people who work full-time should not live in poverty. Even though the minimum wage will rise to $7.25 an hour by 2009, the minimum wage's real purchasing power will still be below what it was in 1968.

The plan will further raise the minimum wage to $9.50 an hour by 2011, index it to inflation, and increase the Earned Income Tax Credit. This will ensure that full-time workers can earn a living wage that allows them to raise their families and pay for basic needs such as food, transportation, and housing.

Supports Affordable Housing Trust Fund

Obama has supported efforts to create an Affordable Housing Trust Fund to develop affordable housing in mixed-income neighborhoods.

Fully Fund the Community Development Block Grant

Obama's plan will fully fund the Community Development Block Grant program and engage with urban leaders across the country to increase resources to the highest-need Americans.

Establish 20 Promise Neighborhoods

In cities across the nation, Obama's plan will create twenty Promise Neighborhoods in areas that have high levels of poverty and crime and low levels of student academic achievement. The Promise Neighborhoods will be modeled after the Harlem Children's Zone, which provides an entire neighborhood with a full network of services from birth to college, including early childhood education, youth violence prevention efforts, and after-school activities.

Ensure Community-Based Investment

Obama's plan is to work with community and business leaders to identify and address the unique economic development barriers of every major metropolitan area. The plan will provide additional resources to the federal Community Development Financial Institution Fund, the Small Business Administration, and other federal agencies (especially to their local branch offices) to address community needs.

RURAL POLICY

Rural communities face numerous challenges but also economic opportunities unlike anything we have witnessed in modern history. President Obama believes that together we can ensure a bright future for rural America. He will help family famers and rural small businesses find profitability in the marketplace and success in the global economy.

His plan will ensure economic opportunity for family farmers, rural economic development, and improved quality of life for rural residents.

Safety Nets for Family Farmers

Obama will fight for farm programs that provide family farmers with stability and predictability. He will implement a $250,000 payment limitation so we help family farmers—not large corporate agribusiness. His plan for rural areas will also close the loopholes that allow mega farms to get around payment limits.

Anticompetitive Behavior and Family Farms

Obama promises to pass a packer ban: When meatpackers own livestock, they can manipulate prices and discriminate against independent farmers. By strengthening anti-monopoly laws and producer protections, independent farmers will finally have fair access to markets, control over their production decisions, and transparency in prices.

Regulate Confined Animal Feeding Operations (CAFO)

To support meaningful local control, Obama's plan will strictly regulate pollution from large factory livestock farms, with fines for those that violate tough standards.

Country of Origin Labeling

Under Obama's plan, country of Origin Labeling will be implemented so that American producers can distinguish their products from those that are imported.

Organic and Local Agriculture

The farming plan will promote regional food systems as well as help organic farmers afford to certify their crops. Crop insurance will be reformed so that it will not penalize organic farmers.

Encourage Young People to Become Farmers

Obama hopes to establish a new program to identify and train the next generation of farmers. He will do so by providing tax incentives that make it easier for new farmers to afford their first farm.

Conserve Private Lands

The plan will increase incentives for farmers and private landowners to conduct sustainable agriculture and protect wetlands, grasslands, and forests. By partnering with the landowners, Obama believes we can conserve private land.

Support Small Business Development

Capital will be provided for farmers who create value-added enterprises, like cooperative marketing initiatives and farmer-owned processing plants. The plan will also establish a small business and micro-enterprise initiative for rural America.

Connect Rural America

Obama's plan will modernize a Federal Communications Commission (FCC) program that supports rural phone service and promotes affordable broadband coverage across rural America.

Combat Methamphetamine

To improve the rural quality of life, Obama will continue the fight to rid our communities of meth, and offer support to help addicts heal.

Healthcare

Medicare and Medicaid reimbursement structures that often give rural healthcare providers less money for the very same procedure performed in urban areas. Obama's health care plan will aim to create fair practices. It will attract providers to rural America by creating a loan forgiveness program for doctors and nurses who work in underserved rural areas.

Education

Under the plan, rural education will be improved by providing incentives for talented individuals to enter the teaching profession, including increased pay for teachers who work in rural areas. A Rural Revitalization Program will be created to attract young people to rural America and retain them. Increased research and educational funding for Land Grant colleges will also contribute to the overall goal.

Infrastructure

Obama plans to invest in the core infrastructure—roads, bridges, locks, dams, water systems, and essential air service—that rural communities depend on.

URBAN POLICY

"Americans work harder than the people of any other wealthy nation. We are willing to tolerate more economic instability and are willing to take more personal risks to get ahead. But we can only compete if our government makes the investments that give us a fighting chance—and if we know our families have some net beneath which they cannot fall."
Barack Obama, "The Audacity of Hope"

As a community organizer on the South Side of Chicago, President Obama learned firsthand that urban poverty is more than just a function of not having enough in your pocketbook. It's also a matter of where you live—in some of our inner-city neighborhoods, poverty is difficult to escape because it's isolating and it's everywhere.

The job across America is to create communities of choice, rather than destiny, and create conditions for neighborhoods where the odds are not stacked against the people who live there. President Obama is committed to leading a new federal approach to America's high-poverty areas, an approach that facilitates the economic integration of families and communities with efforts to support the current low-income residents of those areas.

Obama's plan is ambitious. It aims to strengthen federal commitment to cities, stimulate the economy, improve the quality of life in our cities, reduce crime, and increase security.

Strengthen Federal Commitment to our Cities

President Obama will create a White House Office of Urban Policy to develop a strategy for metropolitan America and to ensure that all federal dollars targeted to urban areas are effectively spent on the highest-impact programs. The Director of Urban Policy will report directly to the president and coordinate all federal urban programs.

Fully Fund the Community Development Block Grant

In the long run, regions are only as strong as their people and neighborhoods. The Community Development Block Grant (CDBG) program is an important program that provides housing and creates jobs primarily for low and moderate-income people and places. President Obama will restore funding for the program.

Do No Harm

President Obama does not support imposing unfunded mandates on states and localities. He strongly supports providing necessary funding for programs such as No Child Left Behind.

Economic Prosperity in our Cities

Thriving innovation clusters across the country like the North Carolina Research Triangle Park and Nashville's thriving entertainment cluster prove that local stakeholders can successfully come together and help reshape their local economies. President Obama's plan will create a federal program to support "innovation clusters"—regional centers of innovation and next-generation industries.

This innovation clusters program will provide $200 million in planning and matching grants for regional business, government, and university leaders to collaborate on leveraging a region's existing assets—from transportation infrastructure to universities—to enhance long-term regional growth.

Job Creation

The federal government has a role to play to ensure that every American is able to work at his or her highest capacity. Obama's plan will double federal funding for basic research, expand the deployment of broadband technology and make the research and development tax credit permanent so that businesses can invest in innovation and create high-paying, secure jobs.

Workforce Training

Obama's plan will make long-term investments in education, language training, and workforce development so that Americans can leverage their strengths, their ingenuity, and their entrepreneurial spirit—to create new high-wage jobs and prosper in a global economy. A critical part of this process is ensuring that we reauthorize the Workforce Investment Act (WIA) and ensure that it strengthens federal investments needed for success in the 21st Century.

Capital for Underserved Businesses

President Obama will strengthen Small Business Administration (SBA) programs that provide capital to women and minority-owned businesses, support outreach programs that help business owners apply for loans, and work to encourage the growth and capacity of these firms. He will strengthen Community Development Financial Institutions

(CDFIs), which are engaged in innovative methods to provide capital to urban businesses.

Public-Private Business Incubators

Obama's plan will support entrepreneurship and spur job growth by creating a national network of public-private business incubators, which facilitate the critical work of entrepreneurs in creating start-up companies. It will invest $250 million per year to increase the number and size of incubators in urban communities throughout the country.

Convert Manufacturing Centers into Clean Technology Leaders

America boasts the highest-skilled manufacturing workforce in the world as well as the advanced manufacturing facilities that have powered economic growth in America for decades. President Obama believes that America is at a competitive advantage when it comes to building the high-demand technologies of the future, and he has promised to nurture America's success in clean technology manufacturing by establishing a federal investment program to help manufacturing centers modernize.

Strengthen Core Infrastructure

President Obama's plan will strengthen our transportation systems, including our roads and bridges. As part of this effort, the plan will create a National Infrastructure Reinvestment Bank to expand and enhance, not supplant, existing federal transportation investments. These projects will directly and indirectly create up to two million new jobs per year and stimulate approximately $35 billion per year in new economic activity.

Improve Access to Jobs

America's families and businesses depend upon workers having reasonable access to their places of employment. If approved, Obama's plan will double the federal Jobs Access and Reverse Commute (JARC) program to ensure that additional federal public transportation dollars flow to the highest-need communities and that urban planning initiatives take this aspect of transportation policy into account. The Obama urban agenda will also help facilitate the creation of new jobs in underserved economic areas, so more low-income urban residents can find employment within their home communities.

Invest in a Skilled Clean Technologies Workforce

Obama's plan will increase funding for federal workforce training programs and direct these programs to incorporate green technologies training, such as advanced manufacturing and weatherization training, into their efforts to help Americans find and retain stable jobs.

Mortgage Interest Tax Credit

Many middle class Americans do not receive the existing mortgage interest tax deduction because they do not itemize their taxes. Obama's plan will lower interest payments for homeowners and ensure that middle-class Americans get the financial assistance they need to purchase or keep their own home. This will be achieved by creating a 10 percent universal mortgage credit that gives tax relief to 10 million Americans who have a home mortgage.

Increase the Supply of Affordable Housing

Communities prosper when all families have access to affordable housing. President Obama supported efforts to create an Affordable Housing Trust Fund to create thousands of new units of affordable housing every year. His plan will also restore cuts to public housing operating subsidies, and ensure that all Department of Housing and Urban Development (HUD) programs are restored to their original purpose.

Improve Livability of Cities

Our communities will better serve all of their residents if we are able to leave our cars to walk, bicycle, and access other transportation alternatives. President Obama plans to re-evaluate the transportation funding process to ensure that smart growth considerations are taken into account.

Control Superfund Sites and Data

Obama's plan will restore the strength of the Superfund program by requiring polluters to pay for the cleanup of contaminated sites they created.

Improve Efficiency of Buildings

Buildings account for nearly 40 percent of carbon emissions in the United States today, and carbon emissions from buildings are expected to grow faster than emissions from other major parts of our economy. It is expected that 15 million new buildings will be constructed between today and 2015. Through the use of innovative measures, President Obama will work with cities so that we make our new and existing buildings more efficient consumers of electricity.

Foster Healthy Communities

How a community is designed—including the layout of its roads, buildings, and parks—has a huge impact on the health of its residents. For instance, nearly one-third of Americans live in neighborhoods without sidewalks, and fewer than half of our country's children have a playground within walking distance of their homes. President Obama introduced the Healthy Places Act to help local governments assess the health impact of new policies and projects, like highways or shopping centers.

Improve Transportation

As our society becomes more mobile and interconnected, the need for 21st-century transportation networks has never been greater. However, too many of our nation's railways, highways, bridges, airports, and neighborhood streets are slowly decaying due to lack of investment and strategic long-term planning. President Obama believes that America's long-term competitiveness depends on the stability of our critical infrastructure. He will make strengthening our transportation systems, including our roads and bridges, a top priority.

Support Local Law Enforcement

President Obama has promised to fully fund the COPS program, which will put 50,000 police officers on the street and help address police brutality and accountability issues in local communities. Obama will also support efforts to encourage young people to enter the law enforcement profession, so that our local police departments are not understaffed because of a dearth of qualified applicants.

Reduce Crime with Ex-Offender Support

America is facing an incarceration and post-incarceration crisis in urban communities. Obama will create a prison-to-work incentive program, modeled on the successful Welfare-to-Work Partnership, and work to reform correctional systems to break down barriers for ex-offenders to find employment.

End the Cycle of Youth Violence

Obama's plan will support innovative local programs, like the Cease Fire program in Chicago, which implemented a community-based strategy to prevent youth violence and has been proven effective.

Address Gun Violence in Cities

Obama's plan will repeal the Tiahrt Amendment, which restricts the ability of local law enforcement to access important gun trace information, and give police officers across the nation the tools they need to solve gun crimes and fight the illegal arms trade.

Obama also favors common sense measures that respect the Second Amendment rights of gun owners, while keeping guns away from children and from criminals. He supports closing the gun show loophole and making guns childproof. He also supports making the expired federal Assault Weapons Ban permanent.

Increase Security

President Obama plans to allocate homeland security dollars according to risk, rather than as a form of general revenue sharing. This means cities that are higher on the list of terrorist targets or that have an increased risk of terrorist attacks should receive more money than those that don't.

Prepare Effective Emergency Response Plans

As our nation witnessed in the Hurricane Katrina crisis and its aftermath, too many localities do not have integrated emergency response plans to handle disasters. President Obama will further improve coordination between all levels of government, create better evacuation plan guidelines, ensure prompt federal assistance to emergency zones, and increase medical surge capacity.

Safeguard Mass Public Transportation

Every weekday, Americans take 34 million trips on public transportation systems to get to work, school and beyond. Obama's plan will insist on greater information-sharing between national intelligence agents and local officials and provide local law enforcement agencies with the everyday tools they need to protect their transportation systems.

Cap Interest Rates on Payday Loans

In the wake of reports that some service members were paying 800 percent interest on payday loans, the U.S. Congress took bipartisan action to limit interest rates charged to service members to 36 percent. President Obama believes that we must extend this protection to all Americans, because predatory lending continues to be a major problem for low and middle income families alike.

Encourage Lenders to Make Small Consumer Loans

Some mainstream, responsible lending institutions are beginning to enter the short-term lending market to provide many Americans with fair alternatives to predatory lending institutions. President Obama plans to work with his Secretary of the Treasury and the Federal Deposit Insurance Corporation to encourage banks, credit unions, and Community Development Financial Institutions to provide affordable short-term and small dollar loans—and to drive the sharks out of business.

COMMUNITY SERVICE

"Your own story and the American story are not separate—
they are shared. And they will both be enriched if we stand
up together and answer a new call to service to meet the
challenges of our new century ... I won't just ask for your
vote as a candidate; I will ask for your service and your active
citizenship when I am president of the United States. This will
not be a call issued in one speech or program; this will be a
cause of my presidency."
Barack Obama, Speech in Mt. Vernon, IA December 5, 2007

President Obama began his career on the South Side of
Chicago, working with a coalition of churches to improve
living conditions in poor neighborhoods. During the election,
people all across the country talked about feeling a new sense
of civic engagement and got involved in politics for the first
time. Now, President Obama is asking Americans from all
walks of life to serve the nation and help address the
problems we face. He's committed to building the
infrastructure and providing the resources that will make it
possible for all Americans to serve to meet the nation's
challenges.

This plan will be executed in several ways:

Expand National and Community Service
Expand AmeriCorps from 75,000 slots to 250,000 and
focus this expansion on addressing the great challenges
facing the nation—helping teachers and students in
underserved schools; improving public health outreach;
weatherizing homes and launching renewable energy
projects; assisting veterans; and helping communities plan,

prepare for, and respond to emergencies. The plan will also improve programs that connect individuals over the age of 55 to quality volunteer opportunities.

Expand the Peace Corps

Double the Peace Corps to 16,000 by 2011. Build an international network of overseas volunteers so that Americans work side-by-side with volunteers from other countries.

Show the World the Best Face of America

Set up an America's Voice Initiative to deploy Americans who are fluent speakers of local languages for public diplomacy. Extend opportunities for older individuals such as teachers, engineers, and doctors to serve overseas.

Expand Service-Learning in Our Nation's Schools

Set a goal that all middle and high school students do fifty hours of community service a year. Develop national guidelines for service learning and give schools better tools both to develop programs and to document student experience.

Expand Youth Programs

Create an energy-focused youth jobs program to provide disadvantaged youth with service opportunities weatherizing buildings and getting practical experience in fast-growing career fields. Expand the YouthBuild program to give 50,000 disadvantaged young people the chance to complete their high school education, learn valuable skills, and build affordable housing in their communities.

100 Hours of Service in College

Establish a new American Opportunity Tax Credit worth $4,000 a year in exchange for 100 hours of public service a year.

Promote College Serve-Study

Ensure that at least 25 percent of College Work-Study funds are used to support public service opportunities instead of jobs in dining halls and libraries.

Create a Social Investment Fund Network

Use federal seed money to leverage private sector funding to improve local innovation, test the impact of new ideas, and expand successful programs to scale.

Social Entrepreneurship Agency for Nonprofits

Create an agency within the Corporation for National and Community Service dedicated to building the capacity and effectiveness of the nonprofit sector.

DISABILITIES

"We must build a world free of unnecessary barriers, stereotypes, and discrimination.... policies must be developed, attitudes must be shaped, and buildings and organizations must be designed to ensure that everyone has a chance to get the education they need and live independently as full citizens in their communities."
Barack Obama, April 11, 2008

Barack Obama's comprehensive agenda is designed to empower individuals with disabilities and equalize opportunities for them. In addition to reclaiming America's global leadership on this issue by becoming a signatory to— and having the Senate ratify—the UN Convention on the Rights of Persons with Disabilities, the plan has four parts, designed to provide lifelong support and resources to Americans with disabilities. They are as follows:

Provide Educational Opportunities
Obama's plan will fund the Individuals with Disabilities Education Act, support early intervention for children with disabilities and universal screening, improve college opportunities for high school graduates with disabilities, and make college more affordable. Additionally, Obama will authorize a comprehensive study of students with disabilities and issues relating to transition to work and higher education.

End Discrimination and Promote Equal Opportunity
By restoring the Americans with Disabilities Act, increasing funding for enforcement, supporting the Genetic

Information Nondiscrimination Act, ensuring affordable, accessible health care for all, and improving mental health care, Obama's plan will allow Americans with disabilities to face fewer obstacles often caused by discrimination.

Increase Employment for Workers with Disabilities

This will be done by effectively implementing regulations that require the federal government and its contractors to employ people with disabilities, providing private-sector employers with resources to accommodate employees with disabilities, encouraging those employers to use existing tax benefits to hire more workers with disabilities, and supporting small businesses owned by people with disabilities.

Support Independent, Community-Based Living

By enforcing the Community Choice Act, which would allow Americans with significant disabilities the choice of living in their community rather than having to live in a nursing home or other institution, the lives of many Americans will improve. Obama's plan will do this by creating a voluntary, budget-neutral national insurance program to help adults who have or develop functional disabilities to remain independent and in their communities, and streamline the Social Security approval process.

Autism

President Obama is committed to supporting Americans with Autism Spectrum Disorders ("ASD"), their families, and their communities. His plan will offer support in four ways:

Funding

Obama's plan will increase funding for autism research, treatment, screenings, public awareness, and support services, as well as research of the treatments for, and the causes of autism.

Life-long Services

For people with autism, the treatments, interventions, and services are an ongoing need, for both children and adults. Obama's plan will improve these services and ensure they are available to those who need them in all stages of life.

Combating Autism Act

Obama has promised to work with Congress, parents, and autism experts to determine how to further improve federal and state programs. Obama's plan would support the funding needed to make the Combating Autism Act a reality.

Universal Screening

Obama's plan will support screening of all infants and re-screening for all two-year-olds (the age at which some conditions, including ASD, begin to appear). These screenings will be safe and secure, and available for every American that wants them. Screening is essential so that disabilities can be identified early enough for those children and families to get the support and services they need.

IMMIGRATION

"The time to fix our broken immigration system is now... We need stronger enforcement on the border and at the workplace... But for reform to work, we also must respond to what pulls people to America... Where we can reunite families, we should. Where we can bring in more foreign-born workers with the skills our economy needs, we should."
Barack Obama, Statement on U.S. Senate Floor May 23, 2007

For too long, politicians in Washington have exploited the immigration issue to divide the nation rather than find real solutions. President Obama believes that the only way our broken immigration system will be resolved is by putting politics aside and offering a complete solution that secures our border, enforces our laws, and reaffirms our heritage as a nation of immigrants.

His plan addresses immigration in five ways:

Create Secure Borders

Protect the integrity of our borders. Support additional personnel, infrastructure, and technology on the border and at our ports of entry.

Improve Our Immigration System

Fix the dysfunctional immigration bureaucracy and increase the number of legal immigrants to keep families together and meet the demand for jobs that employers cannot fill.

Remove Incentives to Enter Illegally

Remove incentives to enter the country illegally by cracking down on employers who hire undocumented immigrants.

Bring People Out of the Shadows

Support a system that allows undocumented immigrants who are in good standing to pay a fine, learn English, and go to the back of the line for the opportunity to become citizens.

Work with Mexico

Promote economic development in Mexico to decrease illegal immigration.

Breinigsville, PA USA
30 November 2009
228360BV00002B/210/P